NAMELESS WOMAN

edited by
Ellyn Peña,
Jamie Berrout,
and Venus Selenite

Published
by the

NAMELESS WOMAN

An Anthology of Fiction
by Trans Women of Color

TRANS WOMEN WRITERS COLLECTIVE

Nameless Woman
Copyright © 2017 Trans Women Writers Collective
www.transwomenwriters.org

First Edition

Cover image: Luvia Montero

This book consists of works of fiction. Names, characters, places, and incidents are either the products of the author's imagination or used in a fictitious manner. Any resemblance to actual events or locales or persons, living or dead, is entirely coincidental.

CONTENTS

BOOK ONE

An Editor's Note   11

Michelle Evans, from *No More Secrets*   17
Vita E., Retrospect   44
Carla Aparicio, Silk, Not Cashmere   50
Dane Figueroa Edidi, The Witches Grey   56
Olive Machado, A Lantern Is Lit   76
DM Rice, Apocryphal   83
Kylie Ariel Bemis, The Sixth World   91
Venus Selenite, Metropocalypse   115
Serena Bhandar, The Root of Echoes   121
Emmy Morgan, from *The Ice Princess*   135

BOOK TWO

Preface to the Original Anthology   151

   Jasmine Kabale Moore, The Girl and the Apple   155
   Joss Barton, Lord, be a Femme   172
   Gillian Ybabez, Lisa's Story: Zombie Apocalypse   178
   Jamie Berrout, Three Fragments   190
   Catherine Kim, Fidelity   201
   manuel arturo abreu, Collecting   210
   Jeffrey Gill, Two Stories   217
   Libby White, Back Home: Three Short Stories   227
   Lulu Trujillo, Space Hunters   239
   Saki, Untitled   250

About the Authors   255

This anthology was made possible by the generous support of hundreds of people. In particular, we would like to thank Annaya Youkai, Kieran Todd, Sadie Laett-Babcock, Adelaida Shelley, Jaime Peschiera, Kai Cheng Thom, Talon Wilde, David Cope, Alex Meginnis, Decklin Foster, and Eli Nelson for their help.

BOOK ONE

An Editor's Note
or, The story of this book

It took us two and a half years to make this book. But it's not that two and a half years of steady work were required to bring this anthology to fruition. The truth is that this book could have been put together in much less time, but the reasons for why this work was fragmented from the beginning, faced delays, and still bears the markings of a rough path has everything to do with the climate in which trans women of color live and why this anthology was necessary for us to create in the first place.

This is a book created by trans women of color to bring together fiction writing by trans women, trans femmes, and nonbinary amab people of color (that is: any person of color who experiences transmisogyny, who is affected by racism as well as the societal hatred of transgender women). Things haven't changed since we first started working on the anthology. A few more trans women of color have been able to publish fiction through small presses lately; and a somewhat larger number of us have managed to self-publish our own work in ebooks or in print. But speaking for myself, I haven't been able to read any of those books; I couldn't afford to read them while we worked on the anthology and I still can't.

And I think this is what moved us to make the anthology: the sense that things would never change, that writers like us would never get their work out there and that we ourselves would never get access to read fiction so striking and relevant as this, unless we published these stories ourselves. But the systemic racism that means nine out of ten editors in the publishing world are white, the quiet white supremacist hearts of those editors who hold multiple liberal arts degrees and reflexively deny equal opportunities to writers of color, the hatred of trans women that's endemic in every quarter and has us on the desolate margins of whatever marginal community we find ourselves at, so that a writer like us among cisgender writers and editors of color still cannot find a place, cannot fit into their exclusive publishing guidelines, their inability to give the support we need to survive while we write, their demands for bland, neoliberal, faux-universal narratives of cishetero POC life, and so on—these forces did much more than just create this vacuum in the literature and drive us toward publishing the anthology.

Consider the fact that two of our editors have had to crowdfund our survival during these past 2.5 years. The fact that more than a handful of our writers have had to do the same, have lacked safe employment and housing and access to health care, among other essential things. That calling out for assistance online has simply been the most visible, public sign of the myriad crises we are faced with in our everyday lives. This is the stuff that gave shape to *Nameless Woman*.

From the beginning, in the summer of 2015, when Ellyn Peña and I began work on the original version of the anthology (BOOK TWO of *Nameless Woman*) we undercut our own ambitions and potential—better that we seek to do little and accomplish at least that than to aim for what we felt was truly needed and fail. We decided to try making a small collection of stories to be published only as an ebook, which would cost and require nothing to produce apart from our own labor.

It went well. The original version of the anthology, released on-

An Editor's Note

line in March 2016, was a success at the very small scale at which we'd been organizing. We sold and gave away several hundred copies, making enough to pay each of our contributors a couple hundred dollars in royalties. It was only after the original anthology had its moment that we at last felt not only moved to do more but could imagine that it might actually be possible—that we really could expand the original anthology (to include the new stories found in BOOK ONE), commission proper cover art to be made, publish the book in print, maybe even get it into some libraries and a bookstore or two, and give the anthology a chance at having a lasting impact.

Just one of the contributors to the anthology had been published by a formal press before, I think. And none of us had a significant audience, literary agents that could get our work looked at by a big publisher, or strong connections to the closed-off world of small press, independent publishing. We had no reason to expect the anthology would be picked up by a publisher—after all, the number of presses in the US that regularly publish work by trans women of color is zero. So we were on our own, in late 2016, in founding the Trans Women Writers Collective, through which we planned to raise funds and publish *Nameless Woman*, as well other books by trans women soon after.

Again, recognizing the radical nature of our work, sensing that the only way we could convince others to support the Collective and help us publish *Nameless Woman* was to set the smallest possible goals and then put ourselves through hell to make things work, we moved forward knowing we could not afford the price of hope.

In raising funds for the publication of the book, having seen other trans women of color in previous years fail to launch their creative projects after missing their initial fundraising goals (it shouldn't need to be said that none of us have the thousands of dollars in spare cash that would eliminate the need to crowdfund our projects), we decided to ask for the bare minimum needed to publish the book and fund the Collective. It was enough to pay each of our contributors a fee of $100, to have the anthology printed, and to give the Collective a chance to publish a second book later on; but we didn't dare ask for the thousands more that would have been needed to pay our editors a fair wage for the hundreds of hours of work we had committed to undertake within a relatively quick deadline.

Everyone loves to see trans women beat the odds, but no one wants to make the profound investment required to help us stay alive. In order to get any sort of help, we've got to smile, possess superhuman strength and be relentlessly positive, take whatever we can get without complaining, and accomplish the impossible. If you don't make it, or if in making it you're so badly wounded that you wish you never tried, it's fine. You'll be scraped off the ground and the next girl will step forward to attempt a death-defying act.

There wasn't a choice, so we set ourselves up to fail. Our editors were to work on the anthology essentially on a volunteer basis for yet another year, and any work turned in after the half year mark was to be considered delayed, a cause for concern (for the life of the book, rather than our own). What's more, thereafter, the slightest difficulty in our health or personal lives, the smallest crisis in our individual economies, meant that work on *Nameless Woman* would come to a halt, sometimes for months at a time. Despite the wonder and joy of being able to work closely with and connect to other trans women of color through writing, the anthology wasn't helping us survive. Materially, it only made life harder.

For my part, after spending a great amount of time on the crowdfunding campaign for the anthology and organizing the book in early 2017, I found myself not only exhausted but also struggling to make rent because I hadn't been focusing enough on doing work that paid. I set aside the anthology and wrote an entire collection of my own speculative short fiction in the first half of 2017, while also relying on freelance editing and sex work, so that I could pay the bills. It wasn't until well into the fall of 2017 that I found myself in a stable enough place to return to the anthology and write these words.

In the preface to the original anthology, we referred to the condition of "permanent crisis" faced by trans women of color—if nothing else, the story of this book is that of crisis: multiple crises, overlapping crises, emotional crises caused by loss and the violence done to us and the people in our lives, recurring financial crises with roots so deep in the interconnected poison wells of capitalism, anti-blackness, white supremacy, and settler colonialism that we can never truly escape them, crises of health which at their least severity still threaten to separate us from our communities and our creative work.

How to wrap our minds around the totality of what we're struggling against? It feels impossible. It might be. But getting to read other trans women, writing these words, giving the anthology over to you, reader—this feels like something.

Maybe a beginning. Maybe a shout that dies in the near distance. But still something.

October 5, 2017
Jamie Berrout

MICHELLE EVANS

Excerpt from the upcoming novella
No More Secrets

"That which can be destroyed by the truth should be."

Grandma says back when she was a kid, folks said that about governments. Corporations. People who traded secrets for power and money. It meant exposing the truth to protect the weak from the powerful.

Hard to imagine that when you see the phrase plastered on government-sponsored billboards.

You hear it on the radio too. "For your safety, remember to synchronize important information weekly. Secrets can only hurt you." I think I was about sixteen when they stopped usin the word "personal" before "information." Tryin to encourage the idea that all information should be public. Race, age, gender identity, sexual orientation, mental health status, blood type, Meyers-Briggs personality profile, childhood pets – people look at you suspicious if they can't see it all at a glance these days. If somebody puts your name in their phone, your whole life story better be there, or you might find yourself getting a visit from the Census Bureau.

Not that you're required to report any of that. They tried to make it compulsory, but a bunch of white people with money got pissy about their constitutional rights gettin violated. So that's when the Census Bureau started callin it a "recommendation", and all the rich white folk celebrated their victory and sipped champagne, not concerned with all the queer black kids living in shitty apartments who got their recommendations in the form of arrest warrants.

So these days, I walk around with my hood pulled low, trying to hide from as many cameras as possible. Normally, there are better ways to stay off camera – Glare, Barcodes, Manyface kits – but those are hard to come by if you don't have the money. But you can't do shit with eyes on you, so that was priority number one. If not for that, there's no way I would have been out here huntin for some crazy, no-face-havin-ass nigga.

…Who I was only going to see so I could hide my face. Yeah, I see the irony.

I was nervous making my way through old town. Not for the reasons people tell me I should be nervous. I wasn't worried about dealers or jackers – they don't bother you if you broke, and I looked plenty broke. And I was just as criminal as they were, truth be told. I was nervous because when all the criminals start sitting in one place, that's where they send the law.

It wasn't hard to find the place once I started looking though. There was only one boarded up old warehouse with a bouncer at the door. He was broad and bald and built like a house. He was sittin in an old lawn chair reading some book, but stood up when I approached. It was like watching a mountain move. I had to crane my neck just to look at him.

I remembered the last message I read before heading out. "Talk to Goliath before you come in. For your own safety." I feel like Goliath didn't do him justice. This man was Godzilla.

"Name?" he asked, in a voice that rumbled through my chest. I swear I felt the concrete shake.

from No More Secrets

"Milo," I answered.

"Where you work, Milo?"

"ATM's. Did the one down 12th last week."

"Word? That was you? Ain't you a little young for–"

"No, I'm not," I cut him off. I hated that question, and being scrawny and short meant I heard it a lot. "You gon' let me in or what?"

"Yeah, in a minute. First I gotta ask, you got any electronics? Phone, tab, watch – even a step tracker in your shoe? Cause none of that is making it inside."

"Nah, I ain't dumb enough to bring any of that here."

He shrugged. "Like I said, I gotta ask." He opened the door and stepped out of the way, but before I could take a step, he stuck out his arm to block my way. "You ain't no cyborg right? No implants, no fakes? I'm not tryna see no more seizures this week."

"No implants, no fakes," I repeated, getting annoyed. I rolled up my sleeves and turned my arms all the way around so that he could see.

He shrugged again and let me pass. As soon as I stepped through the doorway, I felt the familiar buzz that made the hair on the back of my neck stand up. Unfortunately, I also felt the familiar shock of a tick exploding against my thigh.

"Oh shit!"

"Tried to warn you," Goliath said, shaking his head. "You didn't check the strings, did you?"

"You for real? They're putting ticks in the strings now?"

He scoffed. "You ain't know? What kinda hacker are you?"

He didn't wait for an answer before he closed the door on me, presumably to get back to reading. I followed the instructions from last message – down the hall, turn right, down the stairs – and passed through another gate. Thankfully, no shocks this time.

As soon as I reached the basement, I could hear the music – nothing deafening, but the steady thump of the bass would make it near impossible to make out any voices if you were listening from the outside. At the time, I thought taking all those precautions were overkill. Now I'm wishing they'd taken more.

It wasn't the first bazaar I'd been to, but it was definitely the biggest. The whole basement was one wide, open space lit up by shitty old-style bulbs that made the place feel like a gas station bathroom. There were twenty something vendors out with booths and tables set up, and thrice that many shoppers. Most of the vendors were just hustlers trying to unload shit they shouldn't have had in the first place. They were the type who use their real first names in public. Freaks and weirdos, sure, but not the kind I was there to see. I was there to meet Ghandi.

Finding him was a little bit harder. He refused to give me so much as a description over DM's cause he said they were too "hackable." I wouldn't call it hacking when the domain hosts just sell the transcripts to the gov anyway, but that's a quibble. All he would say was "I got the Glare." I had to ask three different people, but eventually someone pointed me in his direction.

If it hadn't been for them, I probably never would have found him. He was posted up in the back corner with black tarps covering most of his set up. You could only see inside through a 2x2 square cut out of one side. Looking in, I could see half a dozen different monitors, but from that angle, I couldn't tell what was on any of them.

"Can I help you?" a voice asked, making me jump. A guy in all black slid up to block the 'window' so quickly I hardly noticed him move. Even inside he had his hood pulled up and a grey visor covering the top half of his face. Paranoid did not begin to describe.

"Yeah. I'm Milo. I hit you up earlier about buyin," I said.

"I remember you. Hold up a second," he said. He disappeared from view again, and I heard him rummaging through containers for about a minute before he came back up. When he returned, he had a shallow, plastic box in hand full of little paper strips, each about the

from No More Secrets

size of a fortune in a cookie. Each one had a unique combination of lines and boxes crisscrossing over the front side. "Ten for ten, cash only."

I picked one up and my whole face turned sour. I took a long, deep breath before I spoke again.

"Nigga. The fuck is this?"

"Fuck you mean? This what you asked for nigga."

I couldn't read his expression with his face covered, so it was hard to know exactly what he was thinking. But I knew that tone of voice well enough to know it only meant one thing. This nigga thought I was a goddamn fool.

"These are Barcodes, nigga! I want Glare! That's the only reason I came out here. Where's the shit I asked for?"

"First of all," he started in a tone that made me want to reach through the window and snatch him up, "I didn't say I was selling Glare. I said I got Glare and I do."

He pointed at his visor for emphasis, and just the bottom half of his face was smug enough to make me want to punch it.

"And second, you didn't ask me for one. You asked me for something to 'get the eyes off me' and these do that. They hide your face from 85% of cameras and they're inconspicuous."

"Nigga, these ain't even the good ones! They're disposable!" I shouted, throwing the one I held back at him. "And what am I supposed to do about the other 15%? Just hope they don't see me?"

I probably would have kept yelling if it wasn't for the hand being placed gently on my shoulder. It was so steady and light I hardly noticed it at first. I glanced down and saw a set of perfectly manicured fingernails curling around my shoulder. My eyes followed the hand and then the arm until I was looking back at a woman in a sharp suit. She must have been at least six feet tall and her hair looked like she'd just stepped out of a salon. Even under this shitty lighting her skin looked like burnished bronze. I'd never met a model in person before, but if I'd seen her anywhere else, I would have known she was one.

For several seconds, I wasn't sure if it was the bass line or my own heartbeat pounding in my ears.

"Is there a problem here?" she asked with a smile. Her voice was warm and light, like honey. With five words, all the anger melted out of me.

"No ma'am, no problem," Ghandi said, suddenly looking squeamish. Apparently he decided that was a good moment to study his feet very intently.

"Are you sure? Because I couldn't help but overhear. It sounded to me like you might have misrepresented some of your wares to a client."

She spoke softly, like a sitcom mom giving a child a mild scolding. But Ghandi looked like he was ready to puke on command. I had a feeling I did not ever want to be on this woman's bad side.

"I'm going to clean up your mess, just this once. But don't let this happen again if you want to continue selling. Understood?"

Ghandi nodded and muttered a "Yes ma'am." I noticed that she didn't say 'continue selling *here*' and it made me wonder just how much pull this woman had.

"Come with me. I'll get you taken care of," she said. She let go of my shoulder and started walking away, her heels clicking on the stone floor. It took another few seconds for my brain to catch up with what had just happened and realize she'd been talking to me.

I leaned forward back towards the little window and hissed, "And you spelled Gandhi wrong, nigga!" Then I turned around and followed the amazon.

"It's stylized, damn it," I heard him grumble behind me. I pretended I didn't.

"Please, have a seat," she said, extending a hand. There were two chairs in front of her desk with their backs to the window that

from No More Secrets

looked like some kind of wooden antiques your grandma buys but no one is allowed to sit in. The one behind it matched, but was twice the size with a high back and cushions in the seat. I took my chair and she took hers.

"You told Goliath you did the ATM on 12th," she said. No hesitation, no wasting time, no question marks. I locked eyes on the painting behind her to avoid eye contact.

"Word travels fast around here, huh?"

"Something like that," she said. A smirk danced on her lips. "I'm surprised. You're a lot younger than I was expecting. What are you, sixteen?"

"Twenty-one," I corrected.

"Ooh, a baby," she cooed. She raised her hand and then closed it, drawing back, as if she wanted to pinch my cheek and then thought better of it. "So what are you doing ripping off ATM's, School Night?"

I fought the blush rising to my cheeks. "I needed the money. And the practice."

"Good answer," she said. She opened her desk drawer and took out a metallic, grey visor, setting it on the desk between us. Unlike the one Ghandi wore, this one was a thin band, only made to cover the eyes. Good enough for what I needed.

"How much?" I asked.

"Sorry, School Night. This one's not for sale," she said. I opened my mouth to protest and she held up a hand, stopping me. I slumped down in my chair. "But I'll let you have it if you're the person I think you are."

"Who do you think I am?" I asked nervously.

She stood up then and crossed the room to lower the blinds. No one could see us and no one could hear us. We were isolated from the rest of the world.

"The person who robbed that ATM also hacked into ten others, along with a gas station, a vending machine, and two public libraries.

The kind of shit any jacker with a dime store trojan could pull off. But they used some very advanced codes to do it. Better than any I've seen in the last forty years, my own excluded."

"Forty years? You barely look forty yourself," I interrupted.

She laughed and it sounded like bells. No, that's not right. Bells wanted to sound like her laugh. "Most people say twenty-nine, but I appreciate your honesty," she said. She took a moment to compose herself before she continued. For the first time since I'd met her, the corners of her lips turned down. "I've seen the thumbprints on all of those hacks. They all share a callsign and it's not Milo."

My heart started pounding again. "You can read thumbprints?"

"That's not even the most impressive thing I can read."

Silence sat in the air for several seconds, weighing me down. She already knew more about me than I wanted anyone to know, and she was digging for more. But leaving wasn't an option yet.

"That was my work," I said.

"I'm highly inclined to believe that. But in my line of work, one can never be too cautious."

"So what you want me to do?"

"I'm not asking for much. I just need you to tell me the callsign you used."

I shifted in my chair uncomfortably. She walked back over, sitting on the desk in front of me and crossing her legs in one smooth motion, the way debutantes do.

"I won't ever tell another soul. I understand the need for secrecy better than most. Believe me, under any other circumstances, I wouldn't be asking you these questions. But there are events in motion that are beyond either of us, and as such, my hand has been forced.

"I'm not gonna hold it against you for hiding your real callsign. I know that when you deal with potentially dangerous people, you have to project a certain image. That's why I have a door man named

from No More Secrets

Goliath. And Milo is a good name for an intelligent, young man with a plan. But this Glare is not for Milo. Nor is the job I have planned. You follow?"

I kept my eyes on the painting. The desk. The carpet. Anything but her as I turned things over in my head. I wondered if maybe this whole thing had just been a set up to get me here. Show off her power, her money, her intel, and draw me into a trap. But I couldn't think of a payoff. If she was Census, then she had more than enough on me to shut me down. And if she wanted to take me out, I'm sure she wouldn't need to put in that much effort.

Up until that night, the goal had always been to stay out of sight and out of mind. Survival. Self-preservation. But something about the way she spoke made me remember my grandmother. The stories she used to tell about protesters. Unions. Civil disobedience. Clashing with the police in the streets. That stuff always seemed like fairy tales to me as a kid.

But I wanted to be a part of them so bad.

"Venus," I answered finally. "That's my callsign. It's short for Venus de Milo."

She nodded and slid the Glare across the desk to me. I picked it up, turned it over in my hands a few times, and then set it back down.

"You still haven't told me who you are."

"Oh! How rude of me," she said. She placed her hand on her chest and shook her head, silently scolding herself. Then she extended her hand to me and smiled. "Call me Athena."

"Bullshit," I said.

She raised an eyebrow, but kept her hand extended.

"Athena's been active for over sixty years. You'd have to be ancient to be Athena."

"I liked it better when you thought I was forty," she said, crossing her arms and frowning. "Listen, School Night, you're smart. Probably a certified genius. But as long as you limit your mind to ignore the things you've been taught are impossible, you're never going to go beyond where you are right now."

It struck me that someone could be so secretive and still wear every emotion so boldly. I hadn't seen her put up any kind of poker face, and the strange thing is, she never needed to. There was just something so incomprehensibly sincere about her that you couldn't see anything beyond whatever she was showing you. That's why, when she told me something impossible, I started to believe it.

"So you're the real Athena?" I asked.

"Only in the sense that you're the real Venus," she said.

"You're being pedantic now."

"I promise, I'm not."

Suddenly, I realized my face hurt. Was I smiling? How long had I been smiling for? That's a bad habit to get into. I gotta cut that out, I thought.

"You said you had a job for me?"

We spent the next hour or so going over the details of what she wanted from me. "A virus that will corrupt massive amounts of data," she said, "but no simple thing. These days, it's not good enough to just delete or overwrite info, the way we used to. There are too many backups, and recovery is too simple now. So I need you to bring me some high quality shit that even the recovery programs will have trouble with."

Her whole demeanor changed once we started talking business. Her tone wasn't harsh, but it was hard – she didn't leave any room to doubt that this was her show and she was allowing me to be a part of it. I may have been her first choice, but if I fucked up, there would be an understudy.

The longer we spoke, the more I got the feeling Athena was playing a game of chess, already looking five moves ahead. She wasn't playing against me, though. I'm not even sure if I was ever a piece on

from No More Secrets

the board. If anything, I think I was the clock. She was just waiting for me to go tick so she could set her plan into motion.

"If you've got any questions, ask them now. You won't hear from me again until the work is done."

"Uh, just one. I'm getting paid for this, right?"

"What, a wink and a smile isn't good enough for you?" she teased. "Don't worry you'll get paid." She opened the door and gestured for me to see myself out. I grabbed my new Glare, slipped it over my eyes and stepped back out into bazaar.

"By the way, School Night?"

I paused.

"If it takes any longer than ninety days, I'm not gonna need it anymore. But I'm expecting you to do it in less."

Over the next few weeks, it was easier to walk with my head held high. With the Glare on, I wasn't worried about the facial recognition cameras capping me. It wasn't gonna fool any human eyes, but with thousands of cameras in the city running 24/7, there was too much camera footage for any organization to search through. Without computer aid, the odds were so stacked in my favor, it would take the intervention of a vengeful god to catch me.

I'll admit, I was cocky. It wasn't just the Glare either. The legendary Athena, the most brilliant programmer of all time said I was a genius. She knew my work and she knew my name. I played every word she said to me again and again. I memorized every moment. Unfortunately, there was one thing she told me that I wouldn't understand until it was too late.

I wasn't in the realm of the possible anymore.

In the stories you always know when you step into something magical. You walk into a ring of mushrooms and the ground opens up. A fairy comes floating down from a star. A creepy little man comes looking for your firstborn. It's all wishes and beanstalks and fast talking.

I just got slammed into a fucking wall.

A rough calloused hand grabbed the back of my neck, pinning me against brick. I hadn't even heard footsteps behind me or seen a shadow in the street. I tried to reach for my pocket, but before I could, another hand grabbed my wrist and wrenched my arm behind my back.

"You getting sloppy, babyboy. If I was a killer, you'd be dead already," a low, raspy voice said.

"Well I guess it's a good thing you just a punk ass bitch, ain't it."

He smacked the back of my head before pulling me off the wall and shoving me away. I spun around to face him, taking a step backwards. At least I was looking at a familiar face, even if it wasn't the friendliest one. Thing is, Patron didn't have friends. But somehow, he managed not to make a single enemy either. Nobody knew enough about him to hate him, and he liked it that way.

But the strangest part was, nobody could describe him. I had a perfect image of him in my mind, but if I were to put it into words, you'd get the completely wrong idea. I can tell you that he wasn't short. He wasn't skinny. He wasn't light-skinned. He wasn't messy. But if I told you he was tall and dark and clean and muscular, you'd start thinking of a whole different dude. And if you tried to describe him to me, I'd have no idea who you meant.

"I keep telling you to watch your back," he said. "One day it might be somebody not so nice catchin you. Cops been real extra lately. Somethin got em jumpy."

"What, that's it? I know you ain't come all the way out here just to give me a warning."

He shook his head and pursed his lip, like he was choosing his next words carefully. "Nah, that ain't it," he said. "Word on the street is you doin work for the Witch."

There wasn't any word on the street. I knew and he knew. But

from No More Secrets

Patron had a way of knowing things he shouldn't. He had a hand in every crime and more eyes than the Census. He was Al Capone if Al Capone paid taxes.

"You know I don't like talking work in public," I said, keeping my voice low. Too many eyes and too many ears made me uneasy.

"Well, right now, I don't give a fuck what you like. Cause you went and talked to the Witch without consulting me first."

"I don't know no Witch," I said.

"Come on, Milo. Don't play dumb. You're too smart to play dumb," he said, sounding disappointed. "Now you might know her by another name, but it's only one job you're workin right now – much to my chagrin."

"Is that what this is about?" I asked. "That I haven't pulled a job for you in a couple weeks? Cause I know my dues are all paid up."

"See, you're just not gettin it. Money ain't the issue – although I do still expect my cut. See, it's like you're my star player and I'm your agent. Your manager. And for you to go talking to the other team without me? That hurts my feelings."

"Well I'm sorry I hurt your feelings," I said, more sincerely than I'd meant to. "But it's not like I went looking for her. She found me."

"Yeah, I'm sure she did. That's sounds just like Glinda. You get dropped off by a tornado and she just happens to be there to make sure you're alright."

The Wiz. That was one of Grandma's favorites. Now he was speaking a language I knew.

"So what you sayin? I shouldn't take the job?"

"Nah, I wouldn't say that. Never let it be said that I would interfere with the free market. But if you're smart, you'll walk away. You're about to get caught up in something bigger than you. And the Witch ain't ever been too concerned with collateral damage."

"Hold up. What you talkin bout?" I asked. As soon as the words left my mouth I mentally cursed myself. I fell for his pitch without even realizing it. But it was too late to backtrack now. "We're talkin about Athena right? 'Power to the People', 'Justice For All' Athena? Who is she hurtin?"

Patron laughed and it made my skin crawl. It wasn't loud. It wasn't shrill. It wasn't quick. It wasn't like bells. "How you think the people get that power? How do you think they get justice? You think they ask nicely? Nah, babyboy. Every revolution has a body count. Athena knows that, and if you get caught up in her game, you will too before long."

"Is that all you think it is? A game?"

"Of course it's a game! It's a game we've been playin since long before you were born."

I shook my head. "If it's a game, what's in it for you? What's the prize if you win?"

Patron raised his arms and turned slowly, gesturing all around us. "I get all this!" he shouted. "I get to keep the status quo just how I like it. See, there's no such thing as a perfect system. Everything we make is gonna be flawed, it's gonna be unbalanced. Even on a chess board, white gets to go first, right? That's all the world is. It's a game where one player has the advantage."

He moved closer to me suddenly, faster than I even noticed, and wrapped his arm around my shoulder. He leaned down and whispered conspiratorially. "But we can cheat. We can work the system back in our favor. We've got the tools, we've got the knowledge. We can take the whole damn kingdom and they'll never even know it. But if we play fair we don't have a chance. History is full of niggas who died playin fair.

"Now, Athena plays fair. She still thinks there's a future out there where everything is equal. Everybody follows the rules and everybody is happy. She wants to build a whole new system that can't be cheated. That wouldn't be so bad if it was just her, but she's got a whole goddamn movement. She gives people hope. She makes mar-

from No More Secrets

tyrs.

"So I'm asking you. Do you wanna be a martyr? Or do you wanna be a king?"

I ground my teeth and took a deep breath. I clenched and unclenched my fists. I don't know why I got so mad hearing him talk like that. It wasn't my cause, I was just getting paid to supply a service. I was just a freelancer. A mercenary if you were feeling dramatic.

But I had a pit growing in my stomach that said he was wrong. I needed him to be wrong.

"I'm going home," I said, shrugging off his arm. "I got work to do. I don't leave a job unfinished."

"That's what I like about you, Milo. You got ethics and principles and shit. Just don't let em get you killed."

I did my best to ignore that. By the time I glanced over my shoulder again, he was gone. Normally I went out of my way to stick to side streets and shortcuts. The less people who saw me the better. But if Patron was still keeping tabs on me, I'd rather not be anywhere so open. So instead of taking the direct route home, I cut through Market Square.

In Market Square, everything was busy at all hours of the day and night. It was four square miles of shops, malls, convenience stores, bootleggers, and street vendors. There were so many food carts out on the street, there wasn't enough room to drive. Sometimes I forgot how many people even lived in the city until I came to Market. But if you wanted to shop legally, this was the only place you could go.

Or if you wanted to get lost in a crowd.

Even the CB's computers have their limits. Put too many FRC's in a place like this, and suddenly you have dozens of overlapping frames, all trying to cap the same faces in the same places. They spend so long sifting through garbage data, they don't ever actually get anything important. It would be like trying to highlight every 'the' in *Harry Potter* by hand.

So the CB leaves the Markets alone and lets local PD take over. Fortunately, all they've got in the area are some old school security drones flying around, running twenty year old software. They were the definition of artificial stupidity. You could fool the things by wearing a white wig and calling yourself George Washington, and that is not an exaggeration. I've seen it done. Anything short of actually pulling a gun somebody and they'll pretty much leave you alone.

If I didn't hate loud noises and bright lights and large groups of people, I'd live here.

Once I was in the Market, I had to slow down, move with the crowd. It wasn't too bad this time of night, so I didn't have to worry about getting bumped and shoved every step I took. But I was assaulted on all sides by the smell. No matter which way you went, the smell of meat and spice and sugar was waiting for you. If I hadn't been hungry already, it would have been enough to get my stomach growling.

I decided to stop by a little bodega, Sofia's, on the way home. It was a place I'd been to before, and I tried to stick to the familiar when given the choice. I grabbed a couple of snacks off the shelf, ordered a sandwich, and went up to the register where I was greeted by a very unfamiliar sign.

NO CASH. CREDIT ONLY.

"Ay, Sofia!" I called out. "Since when you don't take cash?"

Sofia only glanced in my direction for a moment before turning back to the little tv she kept behind the counter. Something on the news about the new Census protocols they'd put in place next month. I'd have to look into that later.

"Where you been at? It's been months since I stopped takin cash, it ain't worth all the extra fees. I don't even keep a register no more."

That wasn't good. It was getting harder and harder to find any place to spend cash. If it wasn't for the bazaars still running downtown, it wouldn't even be worth carrying anymore. If it got much worse, I'd have to find a new line of work. Not much use in stealing money I couldn't spend.

For the time being, I just had to grit my teeth and use a card. I took out my wallet and thumbed through it as surreptitiously as I could. Sam, Michael, and Benjamin had all been burned on ATM scams. Scott was clean, but I wasn't finished with his profile – that one would definitely get flagged. Pamela was ready to go whenever, but I had special plans for her. I put too much work into that one to use it on a sandwich. After about a minute longer than it probably took for a normal person to pay for a meal, I settled on John and handed him over.

Sofia scanned the card and I held my breath while I waited for the Approved light to blink green. When the charge went through, I let out a sigh. My relief must have been visible, because Sofia smiled sympathetically as she handed my card back.

"We've all been there, kid. Just gotta make it til payday, right?"

"Oh, yeah. That's all I'm waitin on," I answered, laughing nervously. I decided to avoid doing any more shopping that night. Two panic attacks in one night was already two over my limit.

I was able to make it back to my apartment without any more trouble. I took a few bites of my sandwich, but my appetite was dead. I tossed everything into the fridge and tried to bury myself in my work. But there was too much going through my head for me to concentrate. I didn't want to think that Patron was right, but I knew not everything he said was wrong. The world was more complicated than that.

It took me sixty days to finish writing the program, and then two weeks after that to test it on an isolated machine. If this was a job for anybody else, I probably would have had it done in half the time, but I wanted to impress. There was no room for mistakes when you were workin for a legend.

The virus was simple enough in concept. Any database you loaded it onto would appear to be wiped completely, but instead of deleting the data, the program hid it. It made every document appear blank and every file size read zero. And while the data was invisible, a random number generator scrambled it all up. Every second it was active it spread, mixing bits and pieces of data together, until it turned everything into a beautiful mosaic of gibberish. It was a tragedy no one but me would ever see it at work.

This is where things got a little wonky though. See, any semi-competent, community college IT admin would immediately run a restore program and load up a backup at this point. Somebody from a higher pay grade might even just chuck the whole computer and boot up a new server. At worst, you're looking at a few hours of downtime while they get everything set up. So I came up with quite possibly the worst solution I could.

Make it look like I put the data back.

I figured, if I could hide the data while the virus tore it to bits, then it shouldn't be all that hard to "fix" it once it had run its course. I was wrong. It was very hard. But the end result was all of the data magically "restoring" itself, while still being completely worthless to anything aside from the naked eye.

Admittedly, I was relying on human error here more than anything. I had to hope that whoever was in charge would look at the uncorrupted corrupted files, say "Everything looks fine here," and move on to something else. If anyone decided to just say screw it and run the repair program anyway, then it was a whole lot of work for nothing. Even if I was exceedingly lucky, this was only ever gonna work once. Hopefully that would be good enough.

When it was ready, I sent word through Ghandi. Apparently Athena didn't use mobiles, social networks, or even oldstyle chat. Anything you wanted to say to her had to be said in person. I didn't

from No More Secrets

even know it was still possible to live like that, but if anyone could make it happen, it was her.

About a week later, I got sent an address down in old town. Not the bazaar, but close to it. There was a date, but not a time, so I decided to show up early. I packed the essentials in my bag, got there a little before noon and settled in about a block away from the meeting place, ready to bolt at the first sign of trouble. It's not that I didn't trust Athena – if she was Athena – but it always paid to be cautious.

The building itself was a pretty inconspicuous one. A little church that used to be a salon that used to be a gym. The plan was to wait until I saw someone going in or coming out before I went over, but the building looked totally dead. I was getting ready to move up for a closer look when the sun went out. I turned around and realized I was standing in the shadow of a mountain.

"You had the right idea, kid, but you gotta commit," Goliath said. "I've been watching since six a.m. From back there." He jerked his thumb over his shoulder and I had to take two steps to the side just to see around him. There was an old, two-door Lincoln parked a couple blocks back, the kind even my grandmother would have called a classic. It didn't even have tinted windows.

"Shit, are you serious? I know Athena likes to keep it low-tech, but does that thing even run?"

"Yeah, it runs. Come on, we got a long drive."

I followed Goliath back to the car and tried to open the passenger door. It was still locked. Goliath climbed in on the driver's side without a word and reached across the seat to lift up some kind of knob on my side. I took that as my cue to try the door again and got in beside him, holding my backpack in my lap. When it didn't close after me I grimaced and tugged it shut.

"Dude, for real? I'm pretty sure even the pilgrims had automatic doors," I said.

"And I'm pretty sure someone without a car doesn't get to complain," he retorted.

I shut up after that and he started driving north. I wasn't surprised to see we were heading out of town. You always hear about people who live off the grid being out in the woods somewhere, and Athena was the definition of off the grid.

"You're going through all this trouble, I'm surprised you aren't blindfolding me," I said.

"I wanted to. Athena told me not to."

Well. You know what they say about questions you don't want the answer to.

The next hour and a half went by in silence. We didn't even listen to any music, although I wasn't really sure this car was able to play it. But when we got off of the highway, it wasn't to go deep into the woods. We drove through some suburban neighborhood, all the houses spaced out in neat little rows. I always thought it was pretty wild that out of all the inventions of the 20th century, the suburb was the one of the few that persisted. But this one was different from any one I'd ever heard of.

Each house was rigged up with satellite dishes, solar panels and mini wind turbines on the roof. They weren't clean or uniform though, like a professional would do. They looked more like someone hooked one up whenever it was needed and then came back to do another one later. Where some houses were set up with just one, others had over a dozen spread haphazardly across the roof.

As we turned down another street, I started to notice other oddities. There were hardly any cars, and most of the ones I did see were old and junky. The lawns were mostly overgrown with weeds and wildflowers, and the ones that weren't had been turned into vegetable gardens. This was nothing like the kind of shit you saw on TV. Finally, we pulled into one of the driveways, and a garage door opened up to let us in. There were two more prehistoric vehicles inside, but these were in much nicer condition than the ones outside. I checked

from No More Secrets

that the little knob on my door was still pulled up and hopped out. I had to wonder how Goliath even fit inside a vehicle that left me feeling cramped.

We entered the house through a side door and made our way towards the basement. It seemed like every room was loaded up with computers, TV monitors, and other gear and it all looked like it was serving some purpose. When we got to the stairs, Goliath nodded for me to go down alone and shut the door behind me.

The basement was nice, set up much like Athena's office back at the bazaar. Nicer than that actually. I'd never met a criminal with such fancy taste. Even this room was outfitted with tech, though. It was the first evidence I'd seen that Athena might truly be a hacker and not just run some hippie communist trapped in the wrong century. Not that I doubted her... much. It was just nice to confirm what I already knew.

She was sitting behind her desk when I came down, wearing a pair of reading glasses and staring at the monitor in front of her. "Please, make yourself comfortable," she said without looking up. I took a seat in a plush looking arm chair in the corner opposite her and waited. A few minutes passed, and she marked a couple of notes on the screen with a stylus, then collapsed the monitor and set her glasses on the desk. "Sorry about that. Just making a few last minute preparations."

"Preparations for what?" I asked, as much out of reflex as curiosity.

"You'll find out shortly," she answered with a smirk. "How do you like my little subdivision?"

"You tellin me you own this whole neighborhood?"

"This one, and the next one over. The developers were nearly finished with the project when suddenly all their investors found themselves facing mysterious financial troubles. Some worm had rerouted all of their funds into the bank accounts of crooked CEO's, there was a huge legal scandal, and that money got tied up for years. They had to abandon the whole project and let the banks take it. Luckily I just happened to be at the right place in the right time to score the whole place on the cheap."

She shrugged noncommittally, but her half-hidden smile told me she enjoyed bragging. I'd wager it's something she didn't get to do often in her position. For people in our line of work, "I just so happened to be there" was like shining a spotlight on yourself, and Athena seemed to love the spotlight.

"So, you got something for me?" she asked. Right back to business.

"I do… but I wanna ask you a few questions before I give it to you."

She raised an eyebrow at that, pursing her lips slightly. "Alright. Go on."

"Do you know Patron?"

"I know a lot of people, School Night. But I can't say that name rings a bell."

"He seemed to know you pretty well. He even had a nickname for you."

She chuckled at that. "Lots of people have nicknames for me. I'm gonna need you to narrow it down a bit more."

"Well the thing is… I can't really describe him."

That gave her pause. The corner of her mouth twitched a bit. She tried to play it off, but it didn't quite work. "What do you mean you can't describe him? You seem pretty good with words."

"I mean, no one can describe him. Trust me, we've all tried, but it just doesn't work. Normally I wouldn't say that out loud, but I figure–"

"You figure that I would believe you. And you're right. I know who you're talking about. I just didn't know he was active around here."

from No More Secrets

She looked distant for a moment, lost in thought. I was surprised enough to know something she didn't that I let her think. Patron had basically been a fixture of the city for as long as anyone could remember. He never tried to hide or lie about who he was. Yet somehow, he wasn't even on Athena's radar.

Then, her eyes suddenly fixed on me. It felt like being pierced through the heart.

"What did he say to you?" she asked, each syllable a dagger.

"He says a lot of things. Mostly a bunch of crap about chess and knowing how to cheat the system. But... he did tell me that you two have been going at it for a long time. And he told me to be careful around you."

"And you trust him?"

"Fuck no. He's a snake, I just don't know what kind yet. But the thing is... Patron never lies. Even under all the riddles and doublespeak, he only says what he believes."

"I'm sure he does. He knows the truth is the only way he beats me."

It was my turn to give her a look, although I'm sure mine wasn't quite as sharp. "You wanna tell me what that means?"

She sighed. "I will. Some day. But not right now, this isn't the time. When I can tell you is that I won't let any harm come to you for as long as you work with me. I keep my people safe."

That didn't put me completely at ease, but it was reassuring enough. I reached into my pocket and opened up my wallet. I took out Pamela and crossed the room to slide her across the desk. Athena picked her up and gave the credit card an appraising look.

"The plastic can make it through a gate without getting fried, and security scans don't normally check wallets. But pocket drives, cell phones, anything with a CPU in it gets pinged." I shrugged. "Credit cards work."

"You really are a genius, School Night," Athena said, grinning like a kid in a candy store. "Assuming what's inside works as advertised."

I reached into my bag and placed a credit card reader on the desk. It was a heavy black box, heavily customized for my work – nothing like the pretty little things you saw on store counters. "I figured you probably wouldn't have one of these."

"You figure right once again. Let's go set this up."

She got up from her desk, put her glasses back on, and moved over to another machine.

"So how does this whole rig work?" she asked.

"Sorry. Trade secret."

That answer just made her smile even wider. "Perfect."

She set up the reader without much trouble and slid the card into place. Then she turned back to the computer and opened up the system files. It took her about thirty seconds to find and isolate the virus before opening it up to review the code.

"How did you do that so fast?" I asked incredulously.

"Just a little trick I picked up," she said. "Oh, this is a nasty little thing. Pretty impressive work."

I took 'pretty impressive' as the highest praise I was going to get at the moment. I would have liked a bit more 'genius' but I wasn't one to be picky.

"So, you think this will do the job?"

"Oh, absolutely. This will be more than sufficient."

Damn. Trending even further towards the negative.

"So, what exactly is the job? If I'm allowed to ask."

"Oh, it's very simple. We're going to crash the Census."

The days after the virus went out were complete chaos. See, y'all might be thinking that fuckin with the Census ain't that big of a deal. Who cares if nobody knows what the average number of children per family is? Or the number of registered voters per district? Or

from No More Secrets

the breakdown of population by age and gender? That's just statistics and shit, they can gather that info again no problem.

If you're thinking that, it's cause you don't know just how big the Census is. Don't feel bad, most people don't. They like it that way. But the truth of the matter is, the Census has a hand in everything from Department of Defense to your favorite music app. Every time you click "I accept the terms of service," you're giving them something, whether you know it or not.

If you do know how big the Census is, then you're probly thinking that one little virus ain't gonna do shit to them, no matter how brilliantly crafted it is. And you would be right. That's why Athena sent 202.

Goliath and Ghandi wrote about a dozen each to tackle different firewalls. Another sixty something came from other hackers from around the world, most of them I'd never even heard of. All the rest came straight from Athena. She said she'd spent the last decade perfecting each and every one. Apparently she started working on them before the Census even took over. She wouldn't tell me if it was just to be prepared, or if she knew what was coming. I decided it didn't matter.

So where does my one little bug fit into that menagerie? I wondered the same thing.

"Trust me. Your work is going to be the centerpiece," Athena said. "The Census has my thumbprint tagged highest priority, so they should waste a good amount of time chasing me around in circles. If a single one of my programs gets through, I'll be amazed. You kids are going to be doing all the real work."

She was right, as usual. While the Census went after her, Pamela slipped through the cracks along with thirty or so other viruses. In the days after, they got picked off one by one, but somehow Pam managed to survive a full week. And by then, the damage had been done.

At first it was small, isolated stuff. All the social networks were a mess – friend lists were completely scrambled, and even if you could tell who was who, half the time messages went to the wrong person. Personal info was totally random too. I pity anyone who tried to get a date with their hometown set to Scorpio and their childhood pet named *Silence of the Lambs*. And that's just the stuff that was legible.

Vita E.

Retrospect

We met at a club a year ago, my hips open and inviting to the beat of the dance floor. I felt his gaze on me from across the room. White hot. Intentional. Every single moment of this was a magnet. But I told myself, "Girl, he ain't gon' want you the way he says he does with his eyes right now. He ain't seen all of you yet." So I keep dancing, but throwing moves in his direction, thinkin' that this Long Island will kick in, I'll be wavy as fuck, get my validation as a badass, and then I'll call an Über home. I came to the club alone tonight anyway, so that's how I planned on leaving the club. The lights were so bright there, strobing hard and heavy, beat pounding into my chest. That's when I felt it. The hands. Big as I thought they were from the bar. His breath, strong and inviting, his . . . Well I'm sure you get what the fuck I mean. But yeah. He wanted me, and I wanted him. We practically fucked each other's brains out on the floor once the beat dropped. I'll set the stage better so it makes more sense.

   Because I'm well, different than most girls I know, he and I were about the same height. I'm in my red lace dress, short and skimpy, spanks shining in the nightclub lights. No shoes, cause I came without em'. My skin shone with sweat and my locs hung low against my bra-less breasts, still very new from all the hormones I'd been on. My lipstick matched, because of course it did, and my hips were fluid, wide, and ready to move. He was wearing a button down, one that he was barely fitting because of how visibly strong he was. His skin showed in some spots: the opening in his shirt, the cut of his jeans, the glistening forehead and face. Brown treasure looking for brown treasure, and he found me, with those huge hands of his. It wasn't hard for him to get my attention, well at least not all of him. We didn't do names at first. We just let our bodies speak for a while. Just let his hands go and my eyes and hips roll for a while.

"Monique."

"James."

Then it happened...

He touched it...

I froze, cause I had just been clocked in a club full of people, by a man with hands strong enough to kill me. I turned, slowly, as if a gun were embedded into my spine, and said, "I'm sorry. I should go."

My attempt to flee was nowhere near as fast as his grip on my arms, and his utter of, "Please don't. It's ok, ya know? Women come in all types of ways, and they're all beautiful."

Y'all I thought I was being punk'd or something. I legit looked for every camera I could find. He looked at me with those brilliant brown eyes, grabbed my face with those hands, strong and soft all at once, and said simply, "It's ok." Those words must have had infernos inside of them, the way I melted into his arms, and into his bed.

"Girl, what are you doing," my body asked me with a warning. I simply said... "Living."

So many dates, so many nights of passionate love, and so many smiles later, I meet his family. BBQs, play dates with the niblings, cooking lessons from his mom, the whole shebangabang, ya know? We'd even moved next to each other, as my compromise for not accepting his co-habitation offer. But literally, same apartment complex, he was 102, I was 103. It was kinda dope in a way; very slumber party and fuck the shit out me type vibes, ya know? It was going fine, shit, better than fine. It was going great! He even touched me, everywhere, and I mean everywhere! Our love making was some of the best, most romantic, and flat out dirtiest shit I'd ever done, and I loved it. I loved all of it. I loved all of him . . . and I thought he loved all of me.

Ya know the bullshit expression, hindsight is 20/20? Well there must have been a filter on my shit, cause everything about him, and his family, was just like that magnet I talked about earlier. Too good to be true, and impossible to back away from. I tried to welcome that moment in though, because I loved it, and girls like me don't get it as much as we deserve. I'm talking movie nights, kinky days, breakfast in bed, blunts, bongs and records, and that's cliffnotes! It was everything I could do not to be under him, and love all that came with it. But there's nothing that could have prepared me for when I got too close, too comfortable. In the end, it was the magnetism, the white hot intentionality, that would eventually take everything from me.

It started with a surprise: a red lace nightie he sent me while I was at work. I knew what that meant because we had done that shit before, and I knew to have it on when I knocked on his door across the way. It was strange though, cause his door was unlocked, and open, and that had never happened before. It was always him waiting for me to knock. He'd open, topless, rippling muscles and sly face, pretending to be shocked I was there, and then rest is wonderful erotic history. This? This was just off.

I walked into a dark apartment, with him just sitting on the couch. He didn't say a word when I walked in, didn't even rise to meet me. I was so confused, I didn't even think to close the door behind me. What happened next makes horror films look like kids shows, and I swear this: if hindsight is 20/20, I would rather have had shitty hindsight so I could have known this was coming.

"Hey baby," was how he finally stood to meet me. Those hands again, they met me too, right at the hips, my red lace hugging the parts of me his fingers couldn't quite reach.

"Hey love! Your door was wide open. I was a little worried—"

"Naw it's all good. Just had some company over."

"Company? You mean me, right?" At this point I'm trying to play intuition off as paranoia, using a kiss as a buffer for my steady increasing pulse. I mean, he had never hurt me before, so I must be trippin, right?

I knew exactly what he meant by "company," after I heard the door slam, and the lights came on. Turns out, his company hadn't left yet.

"Yo, this her?"

"Damn, she as bad as you said she was."

"Bruh, this shit gon' be fun."

I'm not slow to what's happening, but I'm trying to find my way out. I'm easily staring down ten men, all bigger and stronger than me, so I have three options: I can cooperate, I can fight, or I can try to slide my way out long enough to get some help.

"Oh shit. What's up y'all! How you doing! James, if you got your boys over, we can just link up later."

"Oh it's cool, baby. They came here for you."

"For me? Why?" I try to play it off like I don't know the answer, like I haven't met a few of these boys before. But I had, and they all looked at me with that uncomfortable look, a look that made me wish I had followed my gut and went back into my apartment. The same look James gave me now. The difference was that I had never seen it from him, and I wasn't ready.

"Baby, I don't feel good. I should get some sleep, I got work in the morning." I wasn't lying. Sure as shit, I worked in the morning, and I definitely didn't feel good. The looks of all of these men were omens at best, and at worst, I was about to become a statistic that somehow "deserved it." I knew that if I didn't turn to leave now, it wasn't happening.

"I'm goin home, James. Good night."

The same hands that stopped me from leaving the club when we met, were the ones that were stopping me from leaving his apartment. "But we're just getting started. You don't wanna meet my boys? They heard a lot about you." As if this was some sort of cue to them, the men started to crowd the doorway, and block every potential exit I had. Hands began touching me that were not mine, not James' either. I started to cry, and that made it worse. I'd jerk away, and they'd grab me harder. I could feel their fingernails digging into parts of me that James had only ever touched. Their breath, dangerous, their eyes, cold, my heart, pounding like the bass on the dancefloor. There was nothing I could do. My body might as well have said, "I told you so."

"Please, please don't do this. I love you, James. You don't have to do this."

The only words he said out of his mouth, the same ones, the same, now terrifying words; the ones that told me I wasn't making it out of here alive.

As soon as the lights went out . . .

"It's ok."

CARLA APARICIO
Silk, Not Cashmere

Brief was the time we spent apart, yet long enough to be reason for a lucid distance, evident most of all when his skin touched mine.

I met him at home in New York, on one of those nights where the streets acted as a somber replacement for the lack of star-studded skies. We ate and drank and I looked into his eyes and I saw a spark of something I desperately wanted to recognize and grow used to. We walked down streets familiar to me that took shape under a new light: a salsa dance club I often ignored suddenly looked so inviting as I pictured us in it, despite the fact that he would need a new set of feet if he were to dance with me. I wanted my movements to dazzle him as his eyes had me. I wanted to seem proud and grounded in my roots. I wanted to not have hated my origins for so long.

I never did learn to dance. I remember the summer of '99 all the kids from my class were taking traditional dance classes after school. That was the summer I noticed the Guayacán in the backyard blooming for the first time, and the summer I was heartbroken when all the flowers died 4 days later.

It was unpleasant for me to hear the típico playing because the only other times that happened, my father had a drink in his hand.

Silk, Not Cashmere

I went to the classes anyway with the intention of giving it my best. We were at an empty room above the local fire station; my school was small and it had a morning shift and an afternoon shift, so we couldn't practice there because it was always a busy time. Anyway, the firefighters only used that room when they had meetings, which was never, because there were only 3 of them.

My nana went with me and her eyes were gleaming with excitement. She loved to dance and did so at every opportunity she got. Sometimes she would even make up opportunities. She couldn't believe the time had finally come for me to learn to dance típico properly.

They paired us up and a teacher started directing us to do this and that and I remember in one of the movements I got really close to my partner and I felt a slight tingle throughout my entire body that startled me. That night in my room I cried because I thought I was going to have a baby. I never went back.

On that night in the city, however, I wanted to dance. I wanted to shine. I only wished to be of his liking, I only wished for him to see me.

His time in New York was brief, as most people's usually is. He left me with a kiss I could only hold onto for a few weeks before it dissipated, and in its place came the thrilling anticipation of more.

When summer came I packed and flew to him across the ocean, because a goodbye is never as satisfying as a love story, and he held me tight. The changes we'd been through since being apart were tangible but our connection was intact: I could still at any moment look into his eyes and find the truth. I would never have admitted this then but what I loved the most was the person he thought I was. I longed to be that interesting, vibrant force. I wanted so badly to rise to new standards and carry actions that had meaning. I longed for meaning.

The sun graced us with its last rays for the day, or forever. We sat on the top of the building, or the world. As we watched the Berlin skyline our words fluttered away sooner than we would have wanted them to but more always came. I couldn't imagine ever getting enough. He talked about his idols and as I contemplated his lively expressions I noticed I had not been minding any sound he made because, though it might have been unfair, it all made sense in some way that transcended such earthly things as words.

I told him that freedom is an illusion and we will always have oppression, because without the fight to exist, those fleeting moments of liberty would be dull and meaningless. He listened to my irresistibly novel ideas, that I no doubt fished out of a monologue of a teenager explaining his beliefs after getting high once, and nodded.

He asked, was I cold? Did I need anything? I shrugged in response, "A blanket, please? The blue one." He climbed down the ladder to his room and I sat alone in the growing dark of the city, staring at the fading sun.

I stood up and looked down: in the distance there were people, like ants, everywhere. All going one way or the other in endless choreography. I wondered where they were going, if anywhere. I wondered who would be waiting for them, if anyone.

Seeing people from above reminded me how different everything can be depending on where you are standing, and how irrelevant and distant life at ground level can seem when you are away. From above, no one looked all that powerful or different. From above, everyone blended into each other and the lines separating personhood and identity were blurred. Their lives intertwined without them meaning to or being aware of it. Everybody always knowing someone who knows someone who knows someone who knows them. I tried to picture my lines and got dizzy. Looking down, I wondered if maybe that is what God would feel like.

Overwhelmed.

A breeze passed and with it went the hazy smoke I was now exhaling slowly, anxiously into the cold night. I considered how far deep I was and how long it would be until the illusion of who we were came

Silk, Not Cashmere

crashing down. Would I still look at him and find the truth then? Would he respect me if he didn't understand my past? Would all this still make sense to him if I stopped making sense?

A breeze passed and with it went some of my will. I heard footsteps as I turned to look back at the ladder. I turned back and let my gaze get lost in the millions of lights. All the little windows with all the people and their ticking clocks marking their decay. My decay.

Would I respect myself if I stopped making sense to him? If he knew that there are months when I don't get up. If he learned at times my space had come alive in the form of piles of trash and mice and flies and drawn curtains and mirrors covered with newspaper and I couldn't lift a finger to fix any of it. That there was a time in which I looked different, and that I would never be able to bear his children. When he walks out on me, as they do—

Could I stand it?

The scarf I wore had many colors and patterns, and it danced around me, trying and failing to follow the wind's every whim. The funny thing was at the store they had lied to me: it was not made of cashmere, it was made of silk. No, the funny thing was in that moment, tears rolled down my face, and I looked down. I imagined my tears falling all the way down to ground level and wondered what the view would be like from there. I wondered if it would look like it all had been worth it.

Before contemplating an answer I considered a different me: one that right there would look back and see the warm shadow crawling back up the ladder. She would brave words no one was there to hear, she would throw her scarf on the floor, and she would fly. The rush would have made it all worth it, and the rush would have made it all black. I flinched and shook my head as a shiver ran through every vein. The sun was gone but the day was not over.

He sat back down next to me and wrapped a blanket around me. It was not blue as I'd asked, it was yellow. At that moment I smiled, and I was surprised to find that I meant it.

His arm around me started to cleanse my thoughts and in a minute, or a million years, other versions of myself joined the fluttering words flying away, and as I watched them go I was left with the uncertainty of whether I was trusting the right thoughts, but the clock would tick and we would see.

DANE FIGUEROA EDIDI

The Witches Grey: A Prelude to the Anthem of Trees

There is an enormous scream that vibrates through the air. As the Earth collapses. The wind dances, her howl a distinct imagining, a sword, cutting through the fog and wails of the dying. My heart trembles as I attempt to rush to the aid of the women and children who have never known such violence in their lives. And I feel it, the hand of the Crone of Death on my shoulder, I turn to stare into her bony face, and gasp as her delicate features and callous smile reflects back my own features. And the cry of a Banshee can be heard in the distance. Hands, bronze, hold a red string and silvers draping in moonlight slice making the sound of a tornado's hymn.

    And my heart races as my eyes open and my hand fumbles in the darkness to grab the cup of water on my nightstand. I can hear the sounds of jazz being crooned into the night as the City That Never Sleeps seems determined to prove worthy of its title. As my hands shake, I attempt to light a candle whose fire the gentlest of wind quickly quiets.

    My room, smelling of seduction and serenades, is big. I shuffle warm feet towards one of the closets and open the door. There is an altar, whose gaze I do not need to see to know what is placed there. A

Sea Shell, a crystal, some herbs and a statue of Aphrodite clothed in her nakedness. I bow my head low to the ground and my words become a mumble as I cling desperately to symbols of my childhood. Aphrodite was called by my mother Oshun of the Mediterranean, Erzule of Greece. Used to say that Love Goddess is the honey needed to drip something sweet onto the tongue of the world. Said she my Goddess and I must go to her when my heart trembles in fear.

I feel her, filling me, a warmth of a thousand lifetimes, and my hands snatch a piece of paper from the draw and without cease seems to craft a story that has yet to come into being.

THE MORNING

The morning greets me. I am lying prone before the altar pieces of paper adorning the floor. Sleep evaded me throughout the night. The sounds of my own tears striking the floor made enough music to keep me occupied. I stand, my long hair cascading from my night cap, down my back. I bring my robes closer to my chest and creep back into bed. There is a gentle knock on my door.

"Come in." I sigh, no rest for the weary. The door opens and a face as dark as Mother Nyx, when she birthed the universe, greets me.

"Mama," she states, her voice one of the sweetest I have ever heard, "The phone rang."

"Oh?"

"Yeah."

"Tell whoever it is I will phone them back."

"It's you, sister," she says frowning.

I offer her a frown as my heart begins to pace. Wrap my robe a little tighter and journey downstairs into the sitting room, where my girls fill the air with gossip I am too old to bother with. I take the phone into my hand gingerly.

"It took you long enough." My sister's voice was always something akin to a bird bashing its brains against the shore. Not true, but whenever she spoke to me that is what I envisioned in my head.

"Contess," I smile, "I didn't sleep well last night. Forgive me for moving a little slow."

"Oh please," she says. "She is dying. I need you here for the ritual."

"Sister, I can't just uproot my life. What about my girls? Isn't Danielle and her husband there?"

"See," her voice is a cackle. "You know it must be you."

"Traveling is not easy for colored—"

"I don't care."

"Well, I have a business to run and—"

"Know this little girl," her voice growls even as sweetly as it dances, "if you do not make it here. I will send Night Terrors to strangle you while you sleep."

And I can hear her hang the phone up.

FATHER

The sweet smell of gardenia fills the house as my girls still draped in night clothes shift about. I turn to see James, our butler, taller than most anyone I have known, with muscles that peer through his suit and a bald head, approaching. He places my suitcase before me and kneels. I kiss him on the forehead and smile.

"You are tasked with protecting my girls while I am away, James," I coo to him, "My father has many enemies and while I have flown above his ambitions, without me here these men may try his hand by trying mine."

"Mama," the girls groan while James stands and exits the room, "why do you have to go?"

"Aunt Contess is one of the scariest creatures I know. You nor

I would ever wish to try her hand," I say as they embrace me and the doorbell rings. When their tears have fallen on my sweater they disburse.

"Mistress?"

"Yes, James," I say, determined to not allow my makeup to run.

"Your father is here." And my heart sinks into the pit of my stomach. While some would say I am the splitting image of my mother, it is my father whom I am closest too. When my eldest sister discarded me to the wolves, he embraced me, shaped a mind for numbers and helped birth a Titan in the business of the Flesh.

"Bring us some scotch, James," I instruct as I sit on the couch. Embodying opulence.

"I would think my daughter whom I have poured so much into would come greet me at the door and not be sitting here." There is a grin in his voice and without another thought, I rush to him and find myself embraced in enormous arms.

"Daddy, you know I would never not honor you." I tell him clasping his hand and walking him to the couch. He smiles with pale lips. My father born of a white father and a black mother is pale enough to pass for white, something he uses to his advantage.

"Why did you call me with such urgency, Dominque?"

"Contess phoned. Mother is dying and I am needed there."

"Death has finally come to get the old bitch has it."

"Watch your mouth, father."

He smiles and I see a certain sadness at the creases of his eyes. He produces something from his pocket, a sparkling blue bottle, and places it into my hands. A tenderness in his gaze I don't recall ever witnessing, "She always told me to send this back with you when it was her time. I don't know why? But I loved . . . love her and want to honor her wishes."

I hold the bottle attempting to figure out what exactly is in it. It's eerie color warm against my eyes. My father also produces papers and snaps his fingers. And I turn, my heart quickening its pace as a handsome young man steps into the room. And a flash of images rush past my thoughts, things I cannot distinguish, a certain dizziness forces my knees to buckle, "Who is he?"

"Phillip," My father says about the young man with green eyes and curly hair, "He works for me. He will be your escort on the train. I will send papers with him to arrange a car for you from the place where the train stops to your town."

"Father, I . . ."

"You what?" my father says drawing close to my ear, "You're willing to dress as a man and try your hand at going it alone? Men as brown as you have not a chance left to the white devils of this dreaded country. You will need a cover. You'll pose as his secretary. And while I know you like punching men in the face, I would rather you not get your hands dirty. This isn't Bloodston, you can't just punish white people without consequence here."

"Alright father," I tell him placing my head to his own. "Alright."

THE TRAIN

People's eyes find themselves lingering upon my flesh as Phillip and I stand patiently by an awaiting door. A snowfall of white seems to blanket the air. I never really enjoyed public spaces. Phillip is a man of little words . . . well he hasn't spoken one. He's handsome . . . I am enticed by his gaze . . . I digress.

The train arrives clouding the air in a fog as we approach the line, a woman with alabaster skin and deepened freckles turns to say something and Phillip turns his head causing her to still her tongue. We head to the conductor who is about to say something and Phillip hands him papers. The conductor reads and hurries us onto the train. The car is empty, eerie almost as if the sorrows of a million men's hands wept themselves into its workings.

Phillip sits by a window, I can smell his cologne caress my nose. It makes me feel . . . warm. And so, I sit beside him. He turns to me, a question in his eye. If he refuses to speak so shall I, there are more ways to access language than with sound. The train wails as it takes off. And the silence of the ride is as loud as the grin Phillip is fighting from forming on his face.

A NIGHT TIME DRIVE

I have heard people speak sweetly of the train as if it were the greatest thing to ever be created. I come from a family of women who can call fire from the sky, so the train never moved me much. Rather than admire the train, I have studied Phillip, the cut of his jaw, the delicate nature of his face, the invitation of his lips, the reluctant curl of his hair and the uprightness of his back and I have found him divine.

We disembark in a town as white as the station we just left. White people gather close and murmur noticing the "Black secretary" doesn't carry anything but a purse while the "white man" she is with, totes her luggage.

Phillip and I find ourselves outside. There are two cars and a group of young white boys gathering outside of them. Instruments in the backseat of one car.

"Phillip," one calls and I see a genuine smile cross his face. One of the young men rushes to grab the bags as another with blush on his cheeks greets me, holding out his hand.

"We are in the south," I say attempting to conceal a smile, "we shouldn't be so formal."

"I am sorry ma'am," he squeaks, "your father is one of our patrons. We play jazz down here. On our way to a town just past where you have to go."

"White boys who play jazz," I say with a smirk. I want to say something else but I offer them a reprieve, the sun is about to fade and no black person was ever safe in these parts at night.

The night bombards us with her eloquence as we find ourselves on a road that seems to stretch for miles. Soon the flash of a police car comes. It forces us to halt. An officer steps out of the car and approaches, flashing light dancing unwanted on our faces.

"What are you boys doing out this late?" he asks, his words sounding like mush between his thin lips.

"We are a jazz band touring, gotta get to—"

"And who are you?" the officer interrupts, his light invading my flesh.

"She works with our manager."

"I didn't ask you, I asked her," he says with a gleam in his eyes. I have seen this before. I have known the violence of white men. And I do not like it one bit.

My heart doesn't pound. My fingers do not fidget although the air is thick with fear. I turn to him with the sensuality of a serpent, head tilted down . . . just slightly . . . and eyes that have their own endearment of mischief.

"I am his secretary sir," I say, my voice light and a flutter. I point to Phillip who doesn't even acknowledge the presence of the officer.

"Is this true, sir."

Phillip nods.

"Are you dumb?" the officer asks.

"No, sir," one of the boys says, "he can't speak."

"Oh," the officer sneers. "A mute. Well, do you mind me taking this n-"

"Please, sir," I tell him placing my hand to my chest, "I'll go wherever you want to go. Just please don't say that word."

"Well, if you're real good, I might even call you something sweet."

I step from the car as the officer guides me into the woods. When we are out of sight, his hands begin to find themselves grasping at my flesh, his lips clumsy find their way to mine. He is taller than I am by a few inches. And I feel his hands try desperately to hike up my skirt. As he meddles, my body pinned to the tree, my hands ball into fists and strike his neck. Stunned, he falls backward, attempting to speak but unable to. My stiletto meets his feet. As my right leg stretches to his left knee. I spin around him and kick the lower part of his back. Almost dancing in my own delight. My heart is steady, my pulse assured.

"How many black girls have you forced yourself upon? I know the glance of evil when I see it, men like you are turned away from my temple every day. I can't really kill them because my father would be so displeased, but you—" I giggle harshly. "I will have fun with you."

From my purse, I produce a few herbs, I see his hands fumble for his gun. I press my foot against his wrist. I punch him in the throat and force open his mouth with one hand and place the herbs within with the other.

"You don't need to swallow, these are from my mother's garden, she taught me how to handle men like you. And just a little on the tongue is enough to end your life," I watch as his eyes bulge and he begins to convulse. Hands flailing, begging me for help, but I see them, black women like me, more than I thought a man like him could ever know, at the mercy of his savagery and as he dies, Phillip joins me.

"My daddy says you know how to get rid of messes."

He nods. I walk back to the car, the men rush to me fear on their faces, relieved when I emerge. I hand them a flask, "No need to worry, boys, just had some business to take care of. Drink this to calm those nerves."

They quickly drink and get inside the car. Their eyes become heavy as Phillip emerges covered in night. He stares at them and I smile, "They shouldn't have to remember such an unpleasant time as this should they?"

I get into the car and wait.

BLOODSTON

The morning dashes itself upon my face. And I find that we have arrived at a small city near the lake called Bloodston. When I was a child, my mother would remind me that there was a rebellion of enslaved black folk here, that the city was named something else, something that masked the violence the plantation owner enacted on the black people here. She reminded me that the day of the rebellion the stones ran hot with the blood of the white people and were permanently dyed the red color they are now.

The city, once a town, buzzes with the low hum of everyday life. In the far distance, you can see a mansion on a plantation. While it shimmers with its own isolated eeriness, the history is one of intrigue and irreverence. That is in fact the mayor's mansion, although it is owned by my family. We walk eyes adrift on myself and Phillip, glances that remember my elder sister throwing me onto the street. The prodigal daughter has returned, and as my feet touch the banks of the lake that will take me to an island which houses a forest and a manor, I smile.

GREY MANOR

In the middle of the patch of clearing is an enormous mansion sparkling in the kiss of the golden sun. I see maids and butlers scurrying around the parameters. Some with wizened face and delicate grey hair I recognize from when I was a child. They rush to embrace me, touching my face as if a ghost had been returned to them. They ask of Phillip, I simply avoid answering. And the doors to my childhood home open and appearing dripping in white with hair the color of dancing flames and skin that seems kissed brown by the caress of sun. This is Contess. My eldest sister. Once a great beauty, something seems fabricated about her in this moment, but I can't see past the light beaming across her face.

"Tom, Mary," my sister's voice once melodic now holds a sharp edge, "leave Ms Grey be."

"We are sorry, ma'am," they apologize rushing away.

"You are as awful as I remember," I yell to her.

"And you have blood on your hands. You better wash them in Calypso's fountain," she instructs staring down at me. Her eyes slide to Phillip, "And what is that?"

"He works for my father"

"And?"

"He protected me from the evils of white men."

"You never needed a man to ever shield you from that," my sister says with an even tone. "He stays in small house with the male servants."

"He's staying in this house." I say as Phillip and I approach.

"You would dare defile these sacred walls with a man."

"Just because the only men who have a fondness for you are clients doesn't mean you get to tell me what to do," I tell her, ascending the steps.

"He doesn't get his own room," she states, her voice barely above a whisper.

"Fine, he can sleep in my bed with me."

We enter the mansion and beside the door is a small fountain adorned with the statue of a woman who appears to be waiting for someone to return. I bathe my hands in its coolness feeling as if my soul would ascend from my skin.

The house is as I remember. A stairway ascending to the floors above. Light streaming in from every direction. The warmth from the west wing filling the house. I watch as young girls adorned in white dresses holding books and speaking distinctly drift by, ghost amongst my memories. We head to the east wing. Up a flight of stairs to a room much larger than the one in NYC. With vibrant red and whites everywhere. Phillip places the luggage down. Then pulls a chair from across the room by the door and sits down.

"Phillip, I have to see my mother. Please, stay here. I know you are worried, but—"

For some reason, I don't recall him moving and I feel his hands brushing against my own. A certain melancholy expression paints his eyes. For a moment, I find a kind of rest there but eventually have to push away kindness: it's time to see the old woman.

MOTHER

Bathed in waters of the lilies. Adorned in a white robe I ascend the stairs. Walking up, the light blares into the space making it appears as if I am moving towards a heavenly glow. And when I reach the attic door, I open it. A woman as dark as night turns to me and bows quickly rushing out. My mother's room always smelled of perfume and sensuality. Once appealing, something to aspire to, it is now sickly sweet and clings to the air objectively. In the corner is my mother's bed. Candles rest next to her almost appearing to float in the air. I walk to the window and open the blinds. Light dances into the room.

"The reason why it is stuffy in here is because you won't open the window."

"Death wanted to take me, closing the window barred him thus," my mother's voice, broken, enraptured in sorrow, causes my heart to weep. She is beautiful still, my mother, with dark skin and a silken waterfall of black hair, her eyes a speechless silver are as expressive as ever. "I am sorry, I wasn't there to help you fight off your sister."

I grab my mother's hand and place it upon my cheek although it chills me, "Let me warm you mother."

"No," she says, "I am not a vampire and you would be wasting your time. The Death Crone must be paid her due. Did you father give you something?"

I dig into a pocket in my robe and produce the vial. "What is it?"

"Life," she grins. She takes her hand and presses it sweetly against my cheek, "I knew your father loved me best. And you must prove your love to me, you are the Death Crone. You have to perform the ritual."

"No, I can't mama."

"Girl, gird your damn loins," her voice is a deathly hiss, "I wouldn't trust that wretched Contess, or that blubbering Danielle. You loved me, the only one that ever loved me true. They can't wait for me to die so they can get my land. If I weren't so tired I would be committed to haunting their ungrateful asses until I drove them mad."

There is a knock on the door, and it swings open. Danielle has always been the most beautiful of our sisters. With curving hips and a bosom she displays openly, her round face is perfectly shaped and her long hair is always in place. The one thing she has never been is graceful, "Sister!" And her voice never failed to annoy. "I am so glad to see you."

"Oh, shut up, you idiotic sow. Who could have ever imagined that I would birth my own Banshee," my mother mumbles. "Certainly, it's the end. Surely."

I grin but stand to embrace my sister. I place a hand to my lip hushing her.

"Oh! I am sorry!" my sister speaks louder.

And in a matter of moments a bed pan is flying past our heads. "Get out!"

I quickly usher Danielle out of the room and clasp her hand as we walk back down the steps.

"How are you, middle sister?" I ask.

"I am good."

"That warms my heart." And we find ourselves in her room. Larger than my own and decorated in golds and reds. We sit at a round table as she raises a small bell and rings it.

"Bastion didn't come with me," she says, her voice becoming even.

"That is good for him," I reply my eyes closing and opening slowly. "What do you want from me?"

"Do not put me out." Her usually sweet face, sharp, stoic and precise. One of the servants enters and places a cup of tea in front of us. My sister pours us both glasses, her grace a far cry from the clumsy girl I once knew. The tea smells sweet. Too sweet . . . I lift the cup, my arms as expressive as a dance and pour the contents onto her floor. She doesn't react.

I stand as she takes a sip of her tea. The poison was on the rim not in the herbs. No matter.

"You have changed Danielle. We were once so close."

"I was forced to have babies while you were given free rein to traipse up and down the east coast."

"I asked you if you wanted me to offer your daughter to the Trees," I say. Her hand is sturdy, her eyes calm.

"Contess could steal her and make her into one of her acolytes. No sister, I would rather smoother her dead myself."

"Why don't you?" I ask. "If you are angry enough to try to poison me, why not kill your own child?"

And I watch as tears begin to spill from her eyes and yet she continues the ritual of taking a sip of her tea, "Why couldn't you just wear the trousers? You were so selfish."

"No, I am just not you."

As I continue to my journey towards the door. I hear the plate slam on the table.

"He still calls your name in his sleep," her voice breaks. I can feel the air become hot. "That man who mother forced me to lie with every night. Even though I yielded my flesh, even though I have never known another woman's lips again, it is at your feet he places his desires, it's your name on his tongue that is so sweet."

"When you seduced him, because you hated me, I forgave you. When you cast love spells to capture his affections, because you hated me, I forgave you. Do not blame me because what you called unto yourself is as rotten as the intention you called him with."

CONTESS

When I arrive at my door Contess emerges, hands pressed gently on her gown. "What were you doing in my room?"

"I was looking for you," she says gingerly, a callous smile on her face, "I am not Danielle, and I don't partake in left overs."

"Yes," I remark tilting my head slightly, "you always had a certain kind of elitism about you."

"Not all of us have forgotten our pedigree."

"Well, that is something a bitch would certainly know something about," I say with a roll of my eye, "what is it you want?"

"What will you do with the house?"

"Why is everyone assuming she will leave everything to me?" I ask.

My eldest sister sighs, an exhale so expressive one would think she was going to dance.

"You are her favorite."

"What does that even mean," I demand, "You and Danielle continue to act as if being a favorite of our mother garners greater favor."

"I was tied to this house, trapped here, cleaning up her shit. Danielle was able to go about her business, able to become a mother, you were free to go to New York and reconnect with your father, I was trapped here to make sure she didn't destroy everything we have built."

I can feel anger begin to rise, as my chest tightens, "It astounds me that the woman who kicked me out of this home would be so indignant about the responsibility she denied me."

My sister moves swiftly, I never remember her moving so fast, and her face is close to my own. My throat stiffens, and I can see her hand become a fist. "What I did was give you a gift. Freedom. You don't know what it means to hold these secrets, to be the matriarch of this clan. Me kicking you out was a gift. You have a life in New York. You and Danielle both have something I wanted when I was young. My voice once beautiful has become tatters, my nerves are shot. And here you are. A Queen. A Witch who would dare stand tall in the face of the mountain that is me. I gave you that."

I stare at my sister, watching the heave of her chest. To be honest I have never seen her react this way. I know I will inherit the manor, the legacy, most of the money and the responsibility. It is something when I was young I would have given every drop of joy for. It something I would have sacrificed myself to free my sisters from, and I stare at my elder sister now, and finally see past the glamour that clings to her skin. She is weary and something in her isn't as strong as she pretends.

I sigh, "What is it you want, Contess?"

And I see her pause. No one in her life had ever asked her that and even as her hazel eyes burrow into me, I can tell she has never thought to say.

PHILLIP

I enter the room and see a vase of roses on the table. Phillip emerges from the bathroom, a towel wrapped around his waist, water sparkling in his hair. Something in me stirs, but as much as my flirtations can be abundant and though my lovers have been many, to him there is a familiarity I can't explain. I smile sweetly, "You didn't sleep with her, did you?"

He grins and shakes his head, then points to the roses.

"She brought me those?"

He nods.

"Will you teach me how to communicate with you when this is all done?"

Now a cat like grin slides across his face. I nod and then creep into the bed. Finally acknowledging my body aches. Then the door rushes open and I see Contess throw Danielle on the ground before us.

"Say it!" Contess says, fire in her eyes.

Danielle with tears streaming down her face stares up at me and shakes her head.

"Please, let it be, Contess."

"Shut up!"

"I—"

"Now," Contess orders and a loud smack echoes in the air. Contess is about to snatch Danielle by the hair, but I leap from the bed and place my body between my sisters, crouching close to middle sister, draping her in my arms like a mother would a child. Contess is about to raise her hand and strike once again but I see Phillip hold it in midair. "Tell your dog to release me. We may not like one another, even hate, but we do not take the lives of sisters. Such savagery is for white men. The blood of Africa runs in our veins. The waters of this land fills us. We do not kill each other over petty things like jealousy."

"Eldest sister, please," I say, feeling something inside of me breaking, my hands trembling as Phillip lets Contess go, "haven't we hated one another enough? Haven't we fought too long? Haven't we abused one another to last generations? I am the mistress of Poison,

Danielle couldn't kill me."

"Our duty is to each other. We all had a role to play," Contess riles. Her face moves close to our own, "Say it, Danielle, or I will send monsters to destroy you as you sleep."

Danielle screams, tears rolling down her face, "I am sorry. I am sorry."

Contess storms from the room and I draw my sister closer to me cradling her in my arms as she weeps, tears beginning to pour from my own eyes. She wipes her own away and shoves away my arms, "I do not need you to save me."

And I sit on the ground, staring at the door in disbelief, my hands shaking and I feel Phillip drape me in his own, "I wanted to save them. I wanted to free them of this place, but I realize they are already seeped into the walls. They have done everything to keep me from this and I came willing to offer my own happiness in exchange for their own. But these women, they do not want freedom, they simply want to place someone else in their position in hell and they are willing to destroy us all to do it."

DEATH CRONE

I stare at my mother, lights flickering, the air cool outside in the woods. My two sisters have retired, and I stand alone, dressed in night. My mother, beautiful, rests in a casket made of glass. I draw her lips close to the bottle of blue death, and allow her to drink. She murmurs a thank you, and I watch as the liquid heightens the color of her veins. I stand holding her hands as long as I can, until I watch her ghost depart from her flesh. My voice, an owl's entreaty, sings the holy hymns and watches as the morning gives birth to light.

The Witches Grey

THE WILL

To my dearest sisters,

I want you to know how sorry I am for leaving without saying goodbye, but I miss New York terribly. Phillip and I left at first dawn's light although today is the singing of the Will of our Mother. I had hoped that returning in some way would in fact reveal to me that either one of you would have changed in these longs years that drew us apart. I had hoped that healing and forgiveness would have birthed something new in each other, something that would have let us look at one another as comrades and not enemies in this war of blood.

Contess, you were so sad that your womb was closed, while Danielle you were forced to engage in practices that you should have never known. Perhaps we can make right what was broken between us. While I will leave to go to New York, I ask that Danielle you leave your daughter with Contess. Make her the mother of your lineage. Make her the Mother she always dreamed to be. Contess, as the eldest I ask that you give Danielle her freedom to be the type of woman she was destined to be. Mother is dead let us not make her wishes the knife we use to stab one another in the back.

Contess, you hate the world, even as much as you traveled all over acting as a vessel for the Spirits and The Goddess. I believe to force you out of the home you have built for yourself would be like unto treason. Also, recognize the family you have built around you. Those girls are your daughters too. For so long you have lamented your lot when the universe has given you the children you always hoped for. Offer them the love mother never gave you.

I do hope you are not terribly upset with me. But mother revealed the stock market will one day crash and I have daughters of my own to tend to. Be safe in these upcoming times. And if you are in need use the waterways to call me. And trust, I shall answer.

I love you all, more than you could imagine. But I imagine if I stayed, no good would come to any of us. We have always been better apart. I offer distance as a gift. As a boon.

In deep sincerity,
Dominique Grey

OLIVE MACHADO

A Lantern is Lit on the Grave of a Cleric

At first, a held breath
Glowing, a knight of white wool and umber
Before the paw-printed sand and salt, astride a black footed ferret

I had wandered starways into the western weald
Where you rose from the water and cloud, benighted by it
And I was your stranger, then, your shy little cleric

Lamplit pilgrims, we stumbled along our path
And my hand began to wander into yours
And the sonor of your little laugh, to me, became familiar

And now I am lain in your lap
And the world has turned to wax and oil around us
The ferret knight, and I your saltwater cleric

…

On lacquered wood floats a starry cloudscape of dice and paper

A Lantern is Lit

A cleric and a knightess, cast in the basement light, let a weary breath
I rubbed my eyes to stay the late of night, and you smiled at me
    as always

Here, the farthest end of the world, my basement
On another late night whose end I hoped would never come
I slumped into your arms and read

The orb of milk and sugar
Here, cupped in your tired hands
A shimmer from the highest lantern

We stared and blinked like quiet lambs
Until you had this stupid grin, and asked me sweetly,
"A wish?"

It was true
A wish, cast soft into our palms
A gift of whimpered rest from the twenty-sided-die

And all at once there was laughter and kissing
And you, my knight, were so thrilled
And you looked at me and asked "Well?"

That night, cast softly in silver light and paper
We wondered for what we would wish
As I hid in your arms, your "shy little cleric"

I wished for hot chocolate
Because I knew you would think it was cute
And we teased about a hundred silly wishes

But eventually, the wanderway sway
Whispered out from the western reverb,
And we wished for a ship, of salted scent and white sails

As our adventure ended for that night
I called you my knight in shining pajamas
And when we laid to sleep, I was not so sad

...

We fled through the days,
Tracing stars in our silver ink,
And fleeting between chapters on that floating vessel

At morn I would find myself half asleep
And lie upon the rosewood at your feet
My love, my liege

We are, here in these cold airs
The best friends
A knight, a cleric, and a ferret

Yet I often looked back, watching the glittering lines we cut
    through the sky
You told me to look forward, and not to wander
But I think I have lost a little luster

...

The last night of August came
And I laid weak and cried
And then, again, it was gone

A Lantern is Lit

It hurts to sulk here, in the late of August
The death of summer comes to mind
And I think the things you'd tell me not to

That I am not so young anymore
And with each dead season I become more jaded
And it's true, and I'm terrified

I want to be a lucent little cleric
But my crosier has come to chip away
And my youth and my self feel a little too far today

...

In the autumn rot, you fell into the leaf and damp wood, screaming
With a sudden wind it had come, and gone
But too deep has bitten that hissing platinum, and now lain to rest
    was he, your oldest friend

You cried and clutched the fallow soil
"One last chance, that this might save you"
I watched a little lantern flicker in you

And here I saw the ruin of the world
That all our laughter couldn't fix
And had it been now, we would not have had any doubt
    what our wish would be

I ferried you into the blankets
Where you remained for some seasons
"I want him back, my little paladin"

OLIVE MACHADO

By the autumn after it was okay to laugh
And we were here again, in the sky
And I could make you smile again, so we took flight

…

"That's the end?"
I take your hand tightly and mumble yes
That's the end

Suddenly I am not a cleric
You're not a knight
We're just girlfriends who stayed up way too late

It's sad
Like saying goodbye
And I want to cry, but not in a bitter way

So I ask if you would come with me again
Start a new story, fall in love
And you smile really wide, you were thinking the same thing

But this night is still a goodbye, of sorts
You have work tomorrow, or you're too tired to stay up any longer
So the pen and dice are left alone, the constellations of another sky

And in those hours I am too left alone
And it feels like autumn is dying this time
Maybe I'm mourning for the cleric and the knight

A Lantern is Lit

It is bidding a farewell
This glint of heavenway light
And it is a bittersweet thing

...

Along a coast in the West
We met, lonely strangers
A ferret knight and a saltwater cleric

Like lamplight I came to you
And I was not a cleric until I had you to be a knight
But now, a part of me is sinking, despondent that we were never
    kids together

That every breath might be a few years too late
That I am losing too warm a warmth to be your cleric anymore
That I inherited a sad destiny

But I am not made to slumber and cry, am I?
Here, in this wind whipped vessel you wished for me
We can coast along the air and sea, leaving a silver paint to capture
    the sad quiet of the world

And even though we are so often hurt
I may sit by you and lay hands
And you may make me laugh, and call me wife

So I will stumble along the rosewood deck
An awkward cleric, loved by an awkward knight
And I will lay in your lap, and be your shy little cleric
Never mind how heavy the death of August

DM RICE

Apocryphal

We went to see one of those garage operas I had heard so much about. The Marriage of Figaro. Our stalky curator said something about conceits and transformative processes of interpretation. I wasn't listening. My nails dug into the inside of his left thigh in delicate arches as I looked about. On either end of the bleachers beaten forklifts raised an elaborate speaker system toward us. Through a stroke of luck an old flame in the second violin section scored me a free ticket, and I bought his, and showed him the stub when he badgered me about the price. All the musicians were wearing black masks. He was twirling a single finger across the back of my neck. The crowd was exactly what you'd expect. Lots of expensive glasses and flashy haircuts. He bought this cheapshit bottle of white wine that smelled vaguely like vinegar and I had three cans of PBR. Our fumbling about, stealing kisses between interwoven snide remarks and exaggerated cuddles, annoyed a few of the other patrons, but I was too elated to give a shit. The performance wasn't even all that great. He made a point that the military costuming radicalized the whole thing, but didn't add any to the romance—which was the whole *raison d'etre*! I pointed out the pixie cut peacocking about as the flirty Cherubino, and we agreed (s)he was an exceptional sight to see. He poked his tongue out, and gave an invisible squeeze.

We left at intermission. He gave me an ultimatum—where he made it clear he would rather go out to eat than stay and listen to the slightly off key baritones. I almost immediately gave in. The closest diner made us two eggs, grits, and a pancake each. It was the first time I had ever copied someone's order, and his eyes grew wide at my decision, which I tried to play off by saying I wasn't very hungry, looking away across the empty room. Then I put on a few jukebox jams: Wouldn't It Be Nice, Are You Lonesome Tonight, I Walk the Line. He only commented on the last one, to say that he liked the voice, but never listened to his music. I had to hold back to not do the Elvis monologue. Maybe I should have. That would have been funny, right? I probably would have fucked up the words, so I didn't. We hadn't been together for that long.

Act one was when we met: at a poetry open mic in this crusty din of a coffee bar in the gayborhood. The resident goth-poetress had just finished her act and it was my turn. A few stunted language poems that weren't really about anything: husks unraveling indeterminate sentiment—castle paradigm: exaggerated articulation simultaneously fishhooking for companionship and stagelighting the unnerving prospect of the self, isle inlet isotope inversion. Then the emcee got back onstage and made a joke about a poet I didn't recognize. Everyone politely chuckled. As soon as I sat down there he was, with a three-fourths filled glass of wine in his right hand and a neon orange folder tucked under his left armpit. Blue flippy hair with red tips. Round cheeks with a thin neck like the wineglass he held. Pale as the wind. I was drenched in sweat. My right leg shook like a horny dog. I asked why he only brought one glass—wouldn't he want some, too? He said that he was on his fifth, which I said wouldn't do. We sipped from the same cup, comfortably bitter haus vino, at my suggestion. I asked about his hair, a trite, but relevant point, and he had me reach forward and feel the thin dye-treated strands that brushed against my fingers in soft wisps. That was when I knew for sure. We sat in the back corner of that shithole coffee bar and he showed me the poems he had planned on reading that night, before he started drinking; the first one was a dime-a-dozen depression piece, though the second one, something about a super-hero cupcake who changed powers depending on what liner it wore, was pretty amusing. We ended up on the balcony and I gave him a cigarette even though he said he rarely ever smoked, but he seemed drunk enough—and he was in the middle of some question but he got stuck on whatever word it was just so much you would have had to have been there the hesitation on his lips pantomiming after some sound that just wasn't coming: I threw my lips into his and we twirled tongues until the emcee came for us, strutting his hairless legs in fishnet stockings, Judy Garland heels; he said the shop was closed, get lost. So we did. I wanted to go back to his place but he said that his roommate would be there, and that she was a bit temperamental about being around new people. So we headed back to mine. We stopped on the way at this shot bar where he knew the owners. It had a real minimal design, blocky black and white canvases distorted by different colored lights that flashed from some unknown crags in the ceiling. I don't know what we had. I'm not even 21 for another two years (and I'm pretty sure he's younger than I am) so I just pointed at something on the menu and the barkeep made it and it was free so I smiled real bright and threw ten dollars in the tip jar. We had a few, maybe more. As he drove my black bug home, I got real lit up about the story that I had been planning on starting.

"So, right, there're 24 hours in the day. And we waste most of it doing nothing. But the whole point of the city is to bring people together, to provide all these options for entertainment, food, all our quick consumer pleasures; human company is always present and available. So why do people get so lonely? Alright, alright. Here's the gist of it: four six-hour work cycles, everyone works a few days a week, and things are distributed so that everyone has a pretty even shake at things, except there's still probly an elite. I mean, what the fuck are you going to do, instill full communism? And really, what's the difference between a noon to six shift and a midnight to six shift? This way, the city never shuts down. Everywhere's twenty-four seven, and so there's some sense of a numbed utopia. A (dis)utopia, I'm thinking of calling it. With parentheses."

"Isn't that just a dystopia?"

"Not exactly. I mean, in a dystopia, everything's clearly fucked, but in a (dis)utopia, see where the parentheses fit? It would seem like a perfect world, but actually be this really fucked up thing. It's the difference between 1984 and Brave New World. We know Oceania is an awful fucking place to live. But Huxley's... goddamn it—where is that story set?"

"I think it's in London..."

"That sounds right, well we don't really know how fucked that place is until we get some ways through it. Even then, I never found his shit THAT scary. I mean, I see the point he's making, but, fuck, there certainly are worse ways for things to turn out..."

He scanned out the side window, changed lanes, and said, "Marx would've had a field day with a twenty-four/seven work week ... hey, what's this music?"

"You've never listened to the tejano station? It's, like, all I listen to when I drive. I basically grew up on it, whenever I went to my grandparents' place they were always jamming it. Heard once that these accordion players makes notes so fast that it can't be transposed to sheet music. And they're basically all ballads, love songs, ya know?"

He nodded and gave a strained smile.

"Do you mind if I change it?"

I said sure and laid my head on his shoulder as he spun through a left turn. He put it on the classical channel, where a piano quartet blitzed along at some allegro pace, and his humming was mostly in tune.

We both lived by the school, but I was in the dorms. No roommate, it wasn't so bad. At the foot of the bed I was on his lap straddling fingers through his hair elbows on his shoulders. He rested his thumb against my lips. Wait, wait. Before we go any further, I have to tell you something. Yeah? What is it? I'm transsexual. The liquor hit me all at once: nibbled a bit at his ear, squeezed him like a stuffed bear. Alright, cool. That's it? Yeah. That's all I've got . . . that's the best reaction I've ever gotten from anyone. Shut up and kiss me. Hold on, look—you're one of three . . . four people now, that know. You can't tell anyone. Not a soul, not a soul. Then closed eyes back to joined pursed lips pulled up his shirt and saw the stitches first I kissed them to the thought of Joan of Arc burning those bursting pomegranate incisions keyhole drillbit shaped like a smile he told me it seared him without warning his body convinced it was under attack that same doe look in his eyes as his packer came loose and I reached my hand down then fell backwards. My head hit the floor.

The next day we walked about through some formless void and laid down the terms of our affair. He told me he didn't normally do things like he did last night. What was he talking about? I felt lighter, spread thin, coaxed out of my shell, exuding affirmation. That's fine? That's fine. We'll take it slow. He used words like struggling, anti-social, busy. I smiled with sympathy, still sincere, knowing no pain, all failure forgotten. We shared relevant details about our upbringings, exes, outlooks on life. Then we appeared before his building. I curtseyed, held his hand against my mouth, gave him one last squeeze, and walked home.

He didn't show face again for a month or so. There was so much apologizing on his part: for not being able to talk on the phone (voice anxiety), stay over without his roommate freaking out (she still didn't know about us), or visit me at work (you know how it is, schedule conflicts). Even the few times I did see him for lunch, it wasn't the same face, let loose with vulnerability, open to the multitude of possibilities that must be lunged through without hesitation, willing to die, if only to live. He was always checking his phone, in case his roommate needed anything, he said. Her presence had already seeped into my imagination, this medusa, this lioness protecting her pride, this poltergeist howling in the wind. I kept quiet to my friends about him, though he did show up at a party my old fwb Myrna had at his apartment complex. On Myrna's bed we made out and my eyes wandered down to a hidden apology teeming with the shame of a purposefully rolled up sleeve, and I loved him all the more.

So the whole opera thing was my attempt to say that, yes, it's okay, life is hard, for all of us, but I wouldn't lose faith, I wouldn't give up, I'd keep the ends out for the tie that binds. After the diner, I realized that my radio was still set to the classical station, and I set it back to ochenta-ocho punto siete, turned it down a little so I could hear him better. He was going on about how people purposefully misused his name, and his whole coming into being, standing up for himself, dealing with everyone's bullshit. It was really something. I thought back to being put down for that kind of stupid thinking, and that, somehow, it had worked even though it hadn't. Maybe I passed, but it wasn't like I was ever that flamboyant to begin with. I didn't have anything to fear: that's what set me and him apart. It was like he was reliving it, looking over his shoulder for bigots hiding in the backseat. I couldn't pity him, but would have if not for the heavy weight of my affection, this poor, damaged kid, who couldn't control the body he was born in. I grabbed his hand, and let it go to make a right turn into the parking lot. Then it was that terribly short walk back to his building, and he still didn't let me walk him to his door, and I stayed there as long as I could manage, making chatter about

Apocryphal

nothing, stealing kisses, looking into his huge eyes. I had that sort of restlessness in my legs that could only be let out by an aimless walk around campus. I passed the art building, the library, and was making my way toward the open courtyard with the statues of the founders. I hadn't seen anyone, which was weird considering that the courtyard is known for being one of the only spots left that security didn't patrol. No, wait. There was one person—there ahead. I didn't look at him, even though he was looking away. He didn't even seem aware of my presence. That's the greatest sort of compliment you can give someone in the city, right? To not notice them, to let them go about their business unobserved. Even without actively giving him my attention I could make out a few details from my accidental glance: he wore a black and white striped shirt, had black hair in an outdated bowl cut, was crouched over in some sort of contemplative pose, staring into the concrete. I pulled out my phone, even though I had no notifications, and pretended to be busy with a text message. Glanced to the right, at the billboard posts, not reading any of them. Stared up into the sky, at the few stars which we city dwellers were afforded, then back in that stranger's general direction, unable to resist the curious nature of his presence, the timid potential to learn of some unknown facet of the human character in his undetectable contemplations. There was no one there.

KYLIE ARIEL BEMIS
The Sixth World

Viola leans into the mirror as she trims her eyebrows. Both so the tiny hairs fall into the sink and so she can tell how much she has taken off. No sudden movements, or she would be truly fucked. No one wants a girl without eyebrows, she thinks. She stands back to examine her work and check that they're even. Neither too thin nor too thick. Satisfied, she dabs some petroleum jelly on her lips, and smears them to a slight glisten.

Here she is again, naked in her bathroom just after midnight, trying to convince herself she can be pretty, trying to subdue the slow-burning hatred of her body with its fat in all the wrong places and all this inconvenient hair. She bends down and runs a palm along the length of her newly-hairless calf, reveling at its smoothness. She performs this ritual maybe once or twice a month. It's been a while. She will have to clean the bathtub later.

Viola walks out of the bathroom and finds her bag full of secrets at the back of her closet in her bedroom. She is thankful she lives alone, she thinks, as she opens it and pushes aside her other secrets and takes out the clothes she needs for tonight. Living alone is lonely, too, but it allows for more secrets, she thinks. It allows for safety.

Safe in her apartment, she pulls on the familiar white cotton panties, and steps into the gray pleated skirt. Then the white cotton blouse. She buttons each white plastic button slowly, carefully, fumbling with every other button as her fingers' muscle memory keeps defaulting to the wrong side of the buttonhole. Her heart beats faster. She can feel its urgency in her chest, under her nonexistent breasts. Then, Viola slides each of her too-big feet into each of a pair of black over-the-knee socks and pulls them up over her newly-hairless thighs. Simple clothes, but full of danger for her.

Designed for a silhouette she doesn't have.

There is a short hallway in Viola's apartment between her bedroom and the living room, with a mirror at the end of it. She crosses it without looking back. Then, in the dim lighting of her after-dark apartment, she turns and faces herself in the mirror at the end of the hall.

She looks almost real, she thinks.

She sways her hips slightly, admiring how the skirt sways back and forth with her.

She watches her doppelgänger dance on the other side of the mirror, wishing she could be that girl, wishing she could step through and become her. But soon her skin is burning like the surface of a sun, her heart weighs ten tons, and she feels like a child caught in a lie.

Am I pretty now? she thinks.

In answer, her ears flood with the sound of blood rushing to her head.

Am I pretty *now*? Am I a pretty girl *now*? Am I a girl *now*?

#

Vincent clears his throat, which makes a sound like a small explosion in the bare audio studio in which he's standing. His fingers are focused on trying to keep the script he's holding from making any noise. The only other thing in the room is a single microphone. Everyone important is sealed away on the other side of the pane of glass that walls off the next room.

"Whenever you're ready," comes the disembodied voice of a god over the intercom. The director? The casting director? The producer? Whoever it is might as well be a god, he thinks.

Vincent clears his throat again.

"This is Vincent Zuni," he says, "reading for the part of Shinji Ikuhara."

They ask him to be a twelve-year-old boy.

They ask him to be a majestic prince.

They ask him to roar like a titan.

Five minutes later, it's over.

"Thank you, Vincent," says the voice from the other side of the glass.

Vincent thanks them and leaves, still trying to cough up whatever remaining rubble of his dreams is caught in his throat. They won't call him back. They never call him back.

\#

"I swear, the *real* End of the World will *really* happen before I get cast for a role that isn't more background noise," says Vincent. He dares to look up from playing with the ice in his iced coffee to try to read the expression on Delilah's face. It's kind of like a smile, he decides.

"At least you *get* auditions," she says. "I haven't even gotten the call once."

They're sitting outside a coffee shop under the lingering sun of the last days of summer.

"Maybe you should listen to my demo sometime and tell me what you think," she says.

Vincent met Delilah in their last year of college in an auditioning class. They are both refugees in the Lone Star State, aspiring pilgrims in Dallas: the unlikely mecca of voice acting studios. There was an electric *something* about her that attracted him to her right away. It wasn't the blue streak in her jet-black hair, or the Gothic Lolita-inspired clothing she wore, or the *I don't give a fuck* way she carried herself, or the assortment of pins and bling on her bag, or even the *kiss me* shape her lips made when she zoned out and stared off into space. These were affectations. No, it was the way these affectations seemed like a mask she *needed* rather than a mask she *wanted* that drew him to her and made him swallow all his fear and boyish terror and ask her to be his partner when their professor had everyone pair off to role-play in class.

"I'd love to," says Vincent. "I've only been asking you for ages."

"I didn't want you to hear it before. It's embarrassing."

"A shy voice actress." Vincent performs what he thinks is a devilish grin.

"It's different." She looks straight at him, into him. "I *know* you."

Delilah doesn't know him. Not really. Just like he doesn't know her. They've shared secrets, but not everything. Not the everything he wants to share. Of course, he was scared to ask her out too soon after they met. He was too scared to ask her about any boyfriends, either. The first time he was over at her apartment, it was to run lines for a class project. He was browsing her bookshelf while she was in the bathroom. Oh, how his heart ached when he accidentally found *Lesbian Sex: 100 Positions for Her and Her* on her shelf beside her collection of Tolkien. Oh, how embarrassed he was when—driven by some otherworldly curiosity—he took it off the shelf and was caught browsing page sixty-nine when Delilah returned from the bathroom.

"Well, it's my first time having a girlfriend!" she said, red-faced and steam-eared.

Vincent could only smile while holding back laughter at the cuteness of her embarrassment, and holding back bitterness at the jealousy that she was taken.

It was a few weeks after that before they could finally look at each other again without blushing, but it was the first intimacy they shared, and Delilah eventually confided in him. She had never dated another girl before, and her new girlfriend was suspicious of bisexuality. Vincent listened to all of it, and tried to imagine the secret world of girls into which he'd never been privy. Sure, he had a sister, and they talked about things, sometimes real things, but that was different. But really, what he wants is for Delilah to look at *him* with those fire-dripping eyes she must surely use to look at that girl before they kiss. Surely, they kiss. And *more*. Right?

"Hey," she says, glancing away, as if she's just remembered something. "Does it ever really worry you?"

"What?" says Vincent. "Auditions?"

"No. The End of the World."

\#

Of course, like most everyone else on Earth, Viola has heard about the End of the World, that tower they're building out in the Mojave. In photos, it looks like a giant silver lightning rod stretching into the stratosphere. It's supposed to use gravitons to create a portal or a wormhole to a new world, another dimension, or something like that, and they're selling tickets on the first rocket ship to take passengers there. It's being billed as a chance for a new start on the distant edges of space, a new frontier, but no one knows what will be on the other side of the portal, and no one knows what will happen to this side of the portal once it's opened. The scientists building the tower say it will be safe, and a lot of people believe them. Other scientists are placing bets like they did for the Manhattan Project last century.

Some are betting the world will really end.

Viola doesn't know what she thinks will happen, but she wants to believe it will be something amazing. She loves imagining the possibility of leaving this world behind for a new one. A new life. But she could never afford a ticket on the maiden rocket in this lifetime. So sometimes, she simply stares into the western sky at night, where, somewhere beyond the horizon, a tower is being built that can crack the shell of this world.

\#

"I'm sure the world won't really end," says Vincent to Delilah. "I mean, that name is just a publicity stunt, right?"

"What makes you so sure?" She looks back at him and runs a hand through her hair. She starts playing with the blue parts of her bangs, which fall just past her lips.

Vincent takes a long sip of his iced coffee before answering. He isn't sure why he likes this bitter liquid so much. Maybe because it makes him feel more like an adult rather than an overgrown adolescent. He's twenty-four, and the lyrics of Neil Young's "Old Man" have been striking a little too close to home lately. The world can't end just yet.

"You must have seen those interviews with the head scientist, too, right?" says Vincent. "The ones where he talks about the bird and the egg? Something about the egg being the world and needing to destroy a world to be born? Or something like that."

Or something like that. Vincent remembers every detail of those interviews.

"I guess so," says Delilah.

"I'm sure they're just trying to be all existential and poetic. Free publicity."

Vincent sips more coffee, trying to be all existential and poetic.

Delilah puts on her own devilish grin. Some of the blue hair finds its way between her lips and into her mouth. Another tic that kills Vincent with cute.

"That head scientist seems like a super villain to me," she says. "I mean, what's up with those tortoise shell glasses? I didn't even know they still make those." She *mmm's* through pursed lips, which means she's thinking. "I've always wanted to play a super villain," she says. "I hope my first role is a super villain."

"You'd be great," says Vincent, and wonders first if this is another secret, and then if this is actually a compliment or not, but Delilah seems happy to hear it. She glows.

"Thanks," she says. "If I were a super villain, I'd build the End of the World, too."

But Vincent can read the worry through her smile. "The scientists building it are smart," he says. "They're the best. I'm sure if they say it's safe, then it's safe."

"The whole idea still terrifies me," says Delilah. She leans back in her chair. The strands of blue hair fall over her face and she doesn't brush them away. She gets that far-away look that turns her eyes into blue flames and curls her lips into that unconscious-half-pucker thing that makes Vincent want to kiss them. "But still, it's kind of exciting, isn't it?"

\#

In the beginning, there was darkness. The people had tails and webbed fingers. They were covered in slime. They had not yet tasted sunlight. They lived underground in the fourth womb where they could not even see one another. They lived in a world of rawness and dust.

Then the twin war gods came down and told them it was not right. They led the people to a ladder, which they climbed into the third womb, the world of soot, where they still could not see one another. From there, they climbed another ladder into the second womb, full of mist and haze, where the sun's light barely penetrated the pale shadows. From that world of fog, they climbed into a womb the color of dawn. The first and last womb.

The people climbed from there to the surface. The daylight world. The fifth world. The sunlight burned their eyes. The lightning seared off the slime covering their bodies. The twin war gods took knives and cut off their tails and the webbing between their fingers.

Viola knows all of this.

She heard it all as a little boy.

She'd been initiated as a little boy like all her boy cousins.

She knows the twin war gods came as stars. And if, back in those days, the stars could go down underground, then she wonders what kind of cavern the night sky might be. She wonders if the End of the World is another ladder, and this world is another womb.

\#

"Just ask her out already," says Maddie's voice from the other side of his phone.

"She has a girlfriend," says Vincent.

Maddie is Vincent's twin sister who lives on the rez. Unlike Vincent, she moved *back home* after finishing college. Well, not really back home, since they never really lived there in the first place, but, in a way, it was going back home. She's married now, with a husband and a child and a house and community responsibilities and all of those other things that Vincent can't possibly imagine. There is even a second child on the way.

"So what," says Maddie. "Maybe she'll leave her for you. You never know."

He does know. He thinks. But maybe Maddie's right. She's always right.

Maddie is younger by two minutes, but she's always felt like the older one. Back in Albuquerque, she was always the one teasing Vincent and looking out for him. When they were children, she terrified him as much as she loved him. In middle school, when she finally noticed someone was stealing her clothes, he was petrified for a week. When she figured out it was him and he only wanted to wear them, she just shook her head and said "Ask me next time you want to borrow something of mine," before adding "and don't let mom or dad catch you."

He was never brave enough to ask her after that, but it made him realize she loved him.

At some indefinable point, Maddie had become a woman while he still felt like that child.

"Are you coming home for Shalako?" she says.

Vincent is standing topless in front of his hallway mirror smoking a cigarette with one hand and holding his phone with the other. He still has some weight to lose. That sash of fat across his belly is haunting him, mocking him.

It's not so much the fat that bothers *him*. It's just distributed wrong.

It's not that it bothers him.

"I'll try," he says. "You know that time of year is always crazy busy for us at school."

Vincent managed to get a job as an administrative assistant at his college after graduating. Delilah went for the more stereotypical path of waiting tables, but she won't tell him where. "You'd come and visit me and make me too nervous to work," she said whenever he asked. Of course, she was right. Of course, he would visit. It *shouldn't* make her nervous considering she wanted to voice act, same as him, but knowing it would make her nervous lit his blood on fire.

"I keep telling you, you'll never grow up if you don't leave that place," says Maddie.

She's probably right again.

When they were in high school, their class put on a play for their senior year project. They decided on a genderbent version of *The Twelfth Night*. Since they were twins, the class voted to cast Vincent and Maddie as Viola and Sebastian. Of course, Viola being played by a boy, as she had been in Shakespeare's day, was the true intention all along. A man playing a woman playing a man. Vincent wore these layers like a second skin. What was difficult was becoming Vincent again. That was the first time Vincent grew his hair out. For the play. For the role. But for the rest of the year, whenever he wore his hair down, his classmates would tease him and call him Viola. Maddie had started it, but he didn't figure this out until much later, or he would have thanked her. He pretended to be bothered by the name-calling, to make sure they would keep doing it. Those were the rules. The secret rules. It wasn't until he and Maddie went off to separate colleges that he remembered the play had been her idea in the first place. Her secret gift to him. A secret kindness about that which she always suspected but never talked about.

"I had another audition today," he says, ignoring her comment.

"That's amazing!" Maddie practically shouts. He has to hold his phone away from him.

"I think I'll ask Delilah out if I get the part."

"Do it," says Maddie.

But that will never happen, he thinks.

And anyway, he doesn't want to ask her out until he has no more secrets.

"Do it," says Maddie again, "before they finish building the End of the World."

"We'll see."

"You may not get another chance after that," she jokes.

Vincent feels a chill in his skin.

#

In Viola's dreams, she becomes Kołamana, the warrior maiden.

Some say she is the firstborn child of the priest's son and daughter who committed incest, and therefore she is a sibling of the Koyemshi.

Some say she is a young woman who saw enemies approaching in the distance while she was in the middle of putting her hair up, who took her father's bow and arrows to drive them off.

Some say she is a young man who has allowed his wife to dress him as a woman, who, when he sees enemies coming, goes off to fight them still wearing his maiden clothes.

Viola doesn't believe any of these stories. To her, Kołamana is simply Kołamana. She is neither man nor woman, but both. Viola knows this. She feels this. It feels like truth.

Kołamana is captured fighting the Kianakwe.

Some say the Kianakwe represent other, enemy pueblo tribes.

Viola doesn't believe this either.

Viola believes the Kianakwe are a reflection, a mirror, a doppelgänger. Viola believes they represent the other that is also us, but she has no one to whom she can admit this.

Kołamana dances when the Kianakwe dance.

Viola has never seen Kołamana dance, because the Kianakwe dance has never been performed in her lifetime.

Sometimes Viola thinks it would be simpler if she were simply born in the wrong body. She knows some people feel like this. But Viola can't help but think that this body is hers and has been given to her for a reason, so she doesn't want to regret being born with it. She has searched the Internet for the language to make herself real—transgender, bigender, genderfluid, genderqueer, two-spirit—trying to find herself reflected in one of them, but the mirror is foggy and mute and won't tell her anything.

Still, Viola is familiar with that silent, violent agony and cage-terror madness of being trapped in a body that doesn't feel right, and she can't imagine the pain of having to fall asleep every night without the possibility of waking up feeling right again. That's what makes her suffering bearable, along with those rare times when her swaying silhouette in the mirror really looks like the girl she imagines herself to be: it comes in waves. Sometimes she is standing on shore, and sometimes she is lying in the wet sand as high tide washes over her like a shroud. Sometimes the tide will ebb, and she can breathe again.

Sleep is her magic spell that makes the pain go away. She can go to sleep and wake up as a boy again. She doesn't know what this means. She isn't real, she thinks. She isn't the prince or the princess. She is the carriage that turns back into a pumpkin at midnight.

Viola's favorite television series is *Revolutionary Girl Utena*, which is also a story about princes and princesses, but not in the usual way. It's what inspired her to get into voice acting in the first place, even though she knows she will most likely never voice any female roles, and she's still not sure if she's more like Utena or Anthy. She likes to think of herself as Utena, but knows in her heart that she's probably more like Anthy, which is okay with her.

Viola likes Delilah as much as Vincent does, even though she's never actually talked to her in reality without Vincent's voice in between them. Sometimes she talks to her in dreams. She thinks they're falling in love with Delilah, but she's afraid to admit this, like Vincent is, so instead she only wishes it, like a prayer. In the soundtrack of her mind, The Arcade Fire's "My Body is a Cage" is playing on repeat.

Viola sometimes dares to imagine herself with Delilah.

All wet tongues and skin against skin.

She likes to imagine herself and Delilah exchanging turns playing prince and princess and saving each other from the things she doesn't dare to imagine.

#

"She broke up with me," comes the text message from Delilah.
Oh shit. Oh shit.
Vincent is at work when his body goes into shock.
He's sitting at his desk, at his computer, juggling students into new classes which, at this point in the semester, they now need instructors' signatures to enter.
He shouldn't answer it. But it's Delilah. He waits until he finishes the next batch of students so he doesn't appear too eager. More secret rules.
It would be too soon, anyway. To ask her out. Right? She needs time to grieve. He'll ask her out if he gets the role. They still haven't called him back.
"Why? What happened?" he texts her between hummingbird heartbeats.
This is another mask.
Don't be too happy. Don't be too impatient. Don't be too pathetic.
Vincent leans back in his chair and takes a deep breath to try to calm himself. His office is sparsely decorated with personal effects. A photo of his sister's family on his desk beside the computer screen. A coffee mug his sister gave him last Christmas painted with *kachina* dancers. A coffee maker by the window beside a tin of coffee and bags of green tea. Outside the window, students shuffle back and forth from class. They're all wearing masks, he thinks.
The girl with the *eat shit* expression and pink hair, who reminds him of Delilah.
The jock hiding behind a tight shirt and biceps the size of tree trunks.
The frat boy with his popped collar and copy-paste hair.

The kid in the band tee and painted-on hoodie and thick black eyeliner.

The women wearing too much make-up or too little make-up.

The men wearing their privilege on their sleeves.

The boys being boys.

The girls being girls.

It's all a performance, he thinks.

Vincent's phone lights up with Delilah's reply and steals his breath.

"She kept thinking I would cheat on her with a guy or leave her for a guy."

Well shit.

\#

It's true that some people put masks on during Halloween and some people take them off.

The first time Vincent was with another man was two Halloweens ago. He wasn't sure if it was an experiment for his own sake or Viola's, but he knew he had to do it.

He couldn't remember the man's name. They met at a gay bar. The man complimented his hair, and Vincent melted and went home with him. The man played guitar and sang for him before pushing him down on the bed. That night, Vincent let his hair down, and as it splayed out on the bed just like he imagined it would, he felt himself becoming Viola, who tried to be swept away as the man sucked on her nipples, but they were Vincent's nipples and it didn't feel right. She couldn't help but keep remembering that this man saw her as a beautiful boy, and not a beautiful girl. The man kept trying to touch her penis, which kept reminding her it was there, and when she took the man's penis in her mouth, it tasted like dust on Vincent's tongue. When the man fell asleep, Vincent walked home in the early morning twilight before anyone could see him.

Therefore, Viola has never been with a man. Viola has never been with anyone. Her body has, but it was no more real to her than the rest of the stage directions she when she has to play Vincent.

The first time Viola went outside without wearing Vincent was last Halloween.

She went out after dark. She wanted to make people fall in love with her. She couldn't remember the names or the faces of the people who saw her, and counted on the fact that no one would remember hers either. If anyone recognized her, or discovered her secret, she could pretend she was wearing a costume. Her safety was in the masks of other people. She enjoyed this magic spell woven by the masquerade night and the dim jazz lighting of midnight bars. She didn't know what to expect, but at one point, she realized a man was talking to her and wouldn't stop. She tried on that half-smile she'd practiced in the mirror that seemed to *suggest* something, but she wasn't quite sure what. A swipe of tongue across her lips, over her teeth. The man started talking faster, started putting his hands on her and moving them over her part by part, as if claiming territory. Her shoulders. Her arms. Her elbows. Her hands. Her waist. Her hips. Her butt. Viola wondered if this was another kind of magic spell. The powerful and terrifying kind.

This man wants to fuck me, she thought.

This man wants to fuck *a girl*, and that girl is *me*, she thought.

She suddenly felt fourteen.

Viola knew this must be what it is like to be a teenage girl exploring her sexual powers, and realized the reason she still felt like an undergrown adolescent was because she never had a proper puberty. Only now was she learning what other girls had learned. The beautiful and the terrible, and when the man's hands started moving forward, his fingers arcing like lightning bolts across the surface of her thighs, trailing sparks toward the places where they weren't allowed to touch at her center, all the synonyms for "stop" caught in her throat. Instead, she excused herself to the bathroom, only to be confronted by two doors, and she wasn't sure which one she was allowed to open. She held it until she got home.

When Viola flooded into her apartment, she saw a girl in the mirror she didn't recognize.

She collapsed on her bathroom floor, shaking, waiting for sleep.

Someday, she decided, she would use real lip gloss. She would learn the names of other kinds of make-up besides eyeliner and mascara and learn how to use them.

Someday, she would get a real razor with real blades, and she would learn how to use it to shave. She would stop relying on her father's old electric razor.

Someday, she would shop for clothes in a real store, and stop ordering her secrets over the Internet, and having to throw half of everything away because nothing fit right.

Someday, she wouldn't wait until after dark to take off her mask.

#

"Are you okay?" texts Vincent.

He wants her to be okay, but only out of selfishness.

Hordes of students pass in the hallway outside the door to his office on their way to class.

If he wants her to be okay, but only out of selfishness, does that make him a villain?

He enters and confirms another batch of schedules.

His phone lights up again.

"Yeah. I was sick of her bullshit anyway," says the text from Delilah.

This could be perfect.

Vincent considers the constellation of questions he wants to ask.

"Think you'll go back to dating boys?" he texts.

"Maybe," is her response.

Vincent knows his next question is all kinds of wrong. But he has to ask anyway.

"But you still like girls too, right?" he texts.

He turns to stone for the several minutes it takes her to reply.

"What? Are you stupid? Don't be silly. I can't change who I am."

Vincent breathes a sigh of relief. In his mind, he can see her face as she is scolding him. In his mind, she is scowling at him, and something about the furrow in her brow and the flare of her nostrils makes him happy. The way she would bite her lower lip while choosing the right disciplinary words. He should know better, after all. But he's learned better than to trust his own judgment. Already, Vincent is imagining the possibility of Delilah loving him. Already, he is imagining the possibility of Delilah loving the part of him that is Viola. He wonders, if she can love him, then maybe she can show him who he really is under all the masks and the thick stage make-up. She is the spotlight, and he wants to play himself. Whoever that is.

"I guess the timing is right, though," says Delilah's next message, which arrives before he has even typed anything in reply to her last one.

"What do you mean?" he texts back.

"Tomorrow. The End of the World. I wonder what will happen."

\#

Maybe because Delilah is now single, maybe because Vincent wants it this way, maybe because it could be her last chance: Viola is the one walking home tonight.

She has a car, but she prefers walking. She still has the same apartment from when she was a student, which she chose so she wouldn't have to drive.

She's still wearing Vincent's clothes. Boring boy's khakis and a polo shirt. Boring business casual. She hates it. These clothes don't feel right.

Her silhouette on the sidewalk is baggy and manly.

No one sees her. They only see Vincent. She hopes no one talks to her.

In this disguise, Viola walks past the religious fanatics with their rapture signs and the environmentalists with their save-the-world signs and the transhumanists with their singularity signs and the space cowboys with their post-Earth-pilgrimage signs. Some are screaming about the apocalypse. Some are begging for money to buy a ticket to escape all this. It's been this way for months. Like then, even now, the students around her ignore them, walk past them, walk toward the homes and dorms that will probably still be here tomorrow. The semester's first midterms are coming up. Viola wonders how many of them are hoping the End of the World isn't just a bad marketing gimmick. Life goes on.

She is relieved when she sees her apartment complex.

Viola hates being trapped outside in Vincent's clothes. She can't talk to anyone like this.

She walks up the three flights of stairs to her apartment and goes inside.

She performs her ritual. She changes into her clothes. She prepares herself.

When it's dark, Viola leaves her apartment and walks down the three flights of stairs to the street and takes a deep breath and steps outside into the night.

The evening breeze touches her skin, brushes its tiny hairs, makes them stand up, gives her goosebumps, between her legs, beneath her skirt. She savors the feeling. It's late, and the doomsday clock is ticking down for those who care. People are partying or puking or studying or sleeping. No one notices her standing there on the corner of the intersection below her apartment at the hour when the traffic lights change faster than anyone can cross the street.

Red light. Green light.

Viola steps out into the street and crosses the lanes and stands on the median.

She closes her eyes.

She spreads her fingers and lets the air pass through them.

Soon, she will go back up to her apartment and fall asleep and wait to be Vincent again.

Soon, but not now. Now, she wants this. Now, she needs this.

Now and then, a car rushes past her, and she imagines the passengers seeing a crazy girl standing on the median with her eyes shut and fingers splayed. A crazy girl, but a girl.

The wind becomes water, and she is drowning in it.

She is drowning.

Maybe she will let the night erase her.

\#

Viola wakes up to the sound of her phone's ringtone. After blinking away the fog and shaking the dust from her mind, she realizes she fell asleep on the couch in the living room, still wearing her clothes. The world outside is the color of dawn beyond her apartment's window. She looks around for her phone before finding it. She doesn't recognize the number.

"Hello?"

"Hello, may I speak to Vincent Zuni?" says the voice of a god on the other end.

"I—he—"

This has never happened before. Viola doesn't know what to do. Sleep didn't cast its usual spell. She is still a girl this morning. Panic sinks its cold fangs into her arteries.

"Can I take a message?" she says.

There is a pause on the other end.

"Sure," the voice finally says. "Let him know the role of Shinji Ikuhara is his. He should call us back at this number before the end of the day if he wants the part."

"Th—thank you," Viola stammers.

The call ends.

I'll ask her out if I get the role, she thinks.

Viola is radiating light and her veins are filled with fire.

Before thinking about anything else, she taps Delilah's number in her contacts list.

The phone rings once. Twice. Thrice.

"Hello?" comes Delilah's familiar, sweet voice.

"Can I see you?" says Viola.

Another godawful pause.

"Vincent, is that you?"

"Are you free today?" says Viola.

"Depends. When?"

"Now. Soon."

"Now?"

Through the phone, she can hear Delilah thinking at her. Deciding her fate.

"Sure. Not for long, though. I'm heading to the coffee shop for breakfast before work. I have about an hour if it's urgent. I should be there in about five—"

The phone call goes dead. No.

Viola looks at the phone. The phone is dead, too.

At the same moment, everything electric shuts off in her apartment building.

Her lights were already off, but the hum of the wireless router, and the refrigerator, and the phone and tablet chargers, and the sleeping computer, and the air conditioning, and the seemingly-silent stereo speakers, and the fan in the bathroom—all go dead quiet.

A devastating calm descends upon the world.

Then the shouting begins. The sound of metal slamming into metal. Screaming.

She rushes to the window. On the intersection below her apartment, cars are pointed in strange directions: cars still running, out of control, or stopped dead. Cars connected to other cars and on fire and billowing plumes of black smoke.

You may not get another chance.

Her sister's words ring in her ears.

Viola stops only to slip on her shoes and grab her keys. The elevator in the apartment building doesn't work. She rushes down the stairs, taking them two or three at a time. She shoves open the door of the apartment complex and the dawn sunlight hits her, but she isn't scared.

There is no lightning to sear off her slime.

There are no twin war gods to cut off her tail or the webbing between her fingers.

But she is a warrior maiden, and nothing will stop her.

Viola finds her uncle's old car from the rez in the parking lot. It was always an eyesore, but it roars to life at the touch of her key and turn of the ignition.

She calculates in her head. *Five minutes.* Delilah would have been on the highway. Near the exit near the coffee shop. That's twenty minutes away. She can get there in ten.

She drives through the chaos on the streets, dodging the stalled cars and the out-of-control cars and the people driving madly across the road and the people running madly across the road, until finally she hits the highway on-ramp.

The on-ramp is bumper-to-bumper with broken-down cars. Some of them won't start. Some of them will never start again. Viola has no time for this.

She gets out of her car and starts running.

When the cars get too tight, she climbs on top of them.

At the top of the ramp, she scans the highway.

Everyone is standing on top of their cars, looking at the dull glow on the western horizon, rivaling the sun rising in the east. Above the glow loom the dark clouds of an oncoming storm.

Viola spies Delilah's powder blue sedan. There is a female figure standing on top of it.

She's alive.

She's okay.

Viola crosses the ten or twenty car lengths between them in what feels like hours or eons. Delilah is wearing her waitressing uniform. She doesn't immediately look away from the horizon when Viola climbs on top of the car with her. When she does look at Viola, she doesn't say anything for almost a minute. She doesn't smile. She doesn't frown. She doesn't burst into tears, but her mouth does hang open across several heartbeats until she manages to speak.

"Vincent?"

"I—" Viola starts. But she can't finish the sentence. The words won't come. She doesn't know what to say or how to say it. She just shakes her head like a tightening spring.

The sky is becoming kaleidoscopic around them.

After a brief lifetime of fear and doubt, Delilah lets out a sigh that is one part laughter and one part relief and weighs a thousand pounds. A sigh that could be as heavy as Viola's heart. The corner of Delilah's lips curl into two quarters of a grin.

"I'm glad you're here," says Delilah.

Then Delilah takes Viola's hand in hers. Their fingers curl into each other. Their fingertips are tiny flames. Together, they look west toward the End of the World.

"I'm scared," says Delilah. "Maybe the world won't be fine. Maybe we're all doomed."

Viola wants to say *"I'm scared, too."*

But as they stand in the light of the radiant twin dawn, Viola realizes the warmth on the back of her neck is the sun, and the warmth in the palm of her hand is Delilah's.

Viola starts smiling. She starts laughing.

Her laughter sounds like it always does in her imagination and in her dreams.

"Maybe," says Viola. "Maybe this world *won't* be fine. But maybe the next one will be better."

She squeezes Delilah's hand tighter.

<<<<>>>>

VENUS SELENITE

Metropocalypse

The city looked like it was evacuating from an impending storm, but that was due to its trains out of service for the next twenty-four hours. The infrastructure was deteriorating and it was decided to cease all trains for one day and have transit workers at every station to make dents in improving the rails. The trains were always quicker and reliable, but this morning, I, along with many multi-class Washingtonians, were subjected to transporting ourselves by bus. Not an empty one today. Each at capacity, people squishing together as canned vienna sausages.

I sat in a chair to get my hair twisted for ten hours yesterday to sit here for the work commute from hell, dammit.

The workload would be equally stressful. My day was predictable, making dozens of coffees, teas, and chais to help satisfy the District's caffeine intake. Whenever someone asked what I did for a living, I told them I was a caffeine dealer. Never a barista. A caffeine dealer. And they would look at me like I disrupted their biorhythm. I held unto the rail above me. My cerulean twists could not escape the spotlight. My hands could only attach themselves to a rail and my purse. No therapist in sight and I unexpectedly ran out of Ibuprofen the night before. If I caught a headache, it was over. Longer commute, more risk of public anxiety.

A tall and stocky man boarded and paid his fare. I only paid attention to his blurry figure from my peripheral until I heard obnoxious questions.

Hey, you single?... What about you? You single?... Oh, look at you. You gotta be single, for sure.

On a moving vehicle of bodies sitting and standing in discomfort, he chooses to begin the day with harassment. A part of me silently chanted for his presence to not cross my direction, but it was inevitable. I was "loud." I "brought attention to myself." He was going to come over and there wasn't time before I could physically prepare for his Juicy Fruit breath to rest upon my neck.

Man looked me up and down for a bit. My eyes were forward, still like mannequins. Man had questions. Many. I had sniffed several dogs like him before.

You single, sweetheart?
Maybe.
What is maybe?
Maybe I'm single, maybe I'm not. It means "maybe." And I'm not sweet.
Oh, you gotta be with sweet with that blue hair.
rolls eyes
What you doing that for?
I'm not sorry, but I'm allergic to your breed.
I can be a nice dog, for you, until I get off at Franklin Square.
I look like a pet-sitter?

Man got on his knees on the crowded bus and started barking. In my mind, I was apologizing to the passengers that they were witnessing more bullshit, on top of twenty-degree weather and an ocean of traffic.

I Street.

What you say, sweetheart?

The bus has stopped. We are on I Street. Which is where Franklin Square is by. Please fuck off.

I'mma see you tomorrow, precious.

And he left the bus. Motherfucker. We weren't even on I Street. I hoped he didn't have a job because he was going to be more late. There was going to be minimal public spectacle of fetishism tomorrow. At least from him.

There was an empty seat in front of me after the latest round of exits. I sat next to a white woman, looked 50-ish, and gave her a small smile. My lower button came undone on my peacoat. When I touched it, the woman opened her mouth.

Have you found Jesus today?

Oh, no. Not again. Lord have mercy.

Don't take the Lord's name in vain! I'll ask you again. Have you found Jesus today?

I envisioned lighting a Virginia Slims, taking a puff, and putting it out on her white wool coat. She seemed to be the type to scream reverse racism. Instead…

turning politely and flashing a faux smile As a matter of fact, I did find Jesus this morning and He told me I would come across a respectable woman whose skin was like milk. You want to know what Word He gave me? That you could suck my left tit.

That wasn't Jesus, but Satan.

No, I'm pretty sure it was your Jesus. White robe and long brown hair? Yes, it was your imaginary Jesus, dear.

Get out! Come out from the sin! Give it to Jesus!

She placed her hand on my thigh. She was fortunate she didn't place her hot ass palm on my forehead.

Blue hair is not of God! Your sins will be marked! Abominations, they are!

At this point, I'm worthy for YouTube again. It is common to run into interesting characters throughout the District, but that behavior was off the tracks today, just like the trains. While this woman continued to yell religion, irritating me, melting the ears off the surrounding people, I attended myself towards the nearest window. If it wasn't for the chaos, the burning cold, the repulsive matters happening underground, a decent day could have been in store.

And look! She's a transgender! God doesn't like transgenders!

Lady, fuck you, okay?

The bus rolled to a stop and I realized I was alone. The woman's eccentricities were ongoing. No one to my defense, my rescue. Just a painful silence, no matter how much my thick skin showed.

I exited, feeling panic. No need for crowding and violence. And I made a phone call.

Hi, it's Bre… The buses are snails. I'm on my way, but walking is faster… No, I rather walk. People showing their asses to me and I've had enough… I think I'm 20 minutes away. I can walk it… I'm sure. See you in a while.

Exhaling, I began the walk to the coffeehouse, but when I did, my shoe slipped on a piece of sidewalk ice and I landed on my back.

Godfuckingdammit, Bre. Why don't you look where you're going?

I laid on the ground, defeated by morning, until a voice crept up.

Oh goodness! Let me help you up!

I'm okay. It's not a big deal. I can man-…

When I looked up, I noticed an ethereal human in front of me. Their accent was thick and Southern. She was my senior and beautifully melanated. Every ounce of their clothing was embroidered with floral patterns. Actually, resting behind her was a bike with a milk crate of flowers attached at the end.

Are you okay, baby? That was a big swoop! Your bum hurt?

Nah, it don't hurt, ma'am. Thank you.

Wait, let me get that for you. You got some ice back there… There you go. That'll dry in a few minutes.

Metropocalypse

Thank you. Um, what is...
Oh, I'm Teresa the Flower Lady!
How did you know I was gonna ask your name?
You ain't the first person I helped off the ground. I'm 68 years old and I'm old enough to know what questions will come to me.
Well, thank you again, Ms. Teresa. I have to get to work. I'm already running late.
Hold up now, give me a second.
She took a moment to retreat to her crate. One blink, and she was placing a blue chrysanthemum in my hair.
It matches, honey! Now you can have a fabulous day!
I pulled out my phone to see my reflection in the screen and I didn't think I would discover a simple joy amid the indecency. She reached out her hands and I shook both, immensely thanking her.
Now go and make your coffee, girl! Fuck these haters!
How did you know I... Never mind, Ms. Teresa.
Now you get it! I'm all-knowing, child!
I watched her pedal away, watching her flowers bloom. They still moved gracefully when she disappeared from my eyesight.
Okay, I'm going to work. Happier.

SERENA BHANDAR
The Root of Echoes

Few questions in the English language can truly end the world as you know it.

"Do you love me?" he asked, not knowing the answer—unsure if he even wanted to know.

"Is that your son?" they gasped, as their forks and knives fell from their hands to the table and floor.

"Where is he?" she screamed; she shouldn't have waited so long to ask.

Each question is the origin point of vastly different diverging parallel universes, is a forked path in the woods with a multiplicity of exits:

I love you. He's wearing a dress. He's gone home.

You repulse me. Yes that's him, why is he wearing a dress. He's lost in the woods.

There's one more question, one that no one thinks about. A question that everyone asks at many points in their lives, that most people answer automatically, without considering its meaning or implication. A question that has the power to uproot all things from beginning to end.

"Who are you?"

I am never coming back, Gabe wrote. *NEVER never NEVER never never.* He tore the page out, tossed it down to the floor, and stamped his foot on it. His boot left a brown treadmark that blotted the ink.

He sighed, then took a deep breath and tugged the ragged remaining thread of paper out of the notebook's coil and put it, and the torn dirty page, into the garbage.

He raised his pen to the next page and began again.

Hypothesis: I am going insane.

Where am I going? What am I going to do? It feels like part of me is dying. Is that true?

I've lived here over 10 years, and I'm finally able to leave. What's keeping me here?

Nothing.

His eyes flicked back up over the paragraph, snagging on the accidental rhyme. "Nope," he muttered, and tore that page out too. This time he didn't bother to clear out the remains.

Hypothesis: I have finally lost it.

He paused, and looked out the window. It was still dark out, but he could see the neighbouring rooftops laid out flat, like cardboard cut-outs. Behind the houses, the hills rolled and broke like waves beneath the half-lit sky.

He gazed back down at the page.

This, this here is my reason to leave. This is what I've been waiting for. Because of this town, I have gone insane.

My evidence: Everyone else here already has.

Gabe went downstairs and had cereal at the kitchen island. His mom sat across from him on the couch. She faced him, but was focused on her laptop, eyes lit up and blurred by the screen. Gabe coughed once, twice. If she noticed, it did not show. He picked up the still-warm empty mug from where she had left it on the island,

and clattered it against the counter. His mom stopped typing and looked up.

"What?" she mumbled with a yawn.

"Good morning," he stated.

His mom paused, then her eyes darted back to the screen and her hands to the keyboard. "G'morning."

Gabe filled his water bottle from the filter, and then left soon after at 7:30, spiral-bound notebook tucked under one arm. The sun still hadn't quite yet risen, and Fern Crescent was still mostly unconscious. Gabe passed dead houses with leaf-strewn front walks and frosted lawns, stepped across sidewalk slabs riddled with veins of moss, and passed under the bare, low-hanging boughs of the oaks lining the road.

The walk to school stretched long through the town—but not long enough to drive. The town, Timber Ridge, cut a five-kilometre square grid into the mostly-flat, formerly-forested land beneath the Ridge it was named after. It didn't show up on some maps. Even Google had skipped it when they photographed for their Street View application. With rain and cloud as the skies' two weather settings, the town rarely had tourists. Sometimes the sun faded into view on the less overcast days, but those were rare and impossible to predict— lack of a dedicated weather person for the region ensured that.

Gabe's commute cut across town along the two main streets, named Cascade and, unironically, Main. He turned left at the single, blinking red light. As he got closer to school, the houses he passed began to revive and awaken. Engines rattled to noisy life in the next street over, and old wood creaked as doors swung open and feet padded over porch boards.

Timber Ridge was not the town people moved to, to raise children, find a job, or retire. The town's only visitors were the occasional forest biologist or rare Sasquatch hunter, who had to stay at hotels over two hours' drive away in the city.

The town's only educational institution, Border Community School, combined all the grades, shoved them together into six decrepit, chalk-yellow concrete classrooms. It was also the biggest and busiest building in the whole town, but that was because it was also home to the Ridge's lumber museum and the town hall, which had monthly meetings in the gymnasium.

The school halls were empty and smelled faintly of chalk dust. Gabe frowned and checked his phone. 8 a.m. No class yet. School started early in the Ridge, but most of the students got there just before the start of class. Socializing was a pastime kept to after school and weekends. By grade 12, it seemed to involve making out, getting drunk, and Gabe didn't want to know what else. He didn't take part in social life in the Ridge, partly out of boredom, partly because he was never asked to join, but mostly because solitude suited him just fine, and all his classmates knew it.

He looked around the hall. There was 20 minutes until the first class, but still, there should have been at least one other person in the school.

"Mr. Mears?" a voice called out behind him. He flinched and turned around at the sound of his name, then sighed.

Ms. Plum, the new school counsellor—an aberration to the town's no visitors—stood outside her office, flicking her fingers up at him in a gesture that was halfway between a beckon and a wave. It was obvious what she wanted to talk about. Graduation was just a couple months away, university acceptance and rejection letters were in the mail, and Gabe had been avoiding her all semester.

"Good morning, Mr. Mears," she began, as he stepped into her office. "Are you having a good morning?" The way she made eye contact on the "you," her irises glinting, unsettled him.

The entire conversation, in fact, was unsettling. Ms. Plum spoke in a very familiar tone—she acted like the two of them had talked many times before.

"Well, my dear?" she asked as she sat at her desk, leaving him standing on the other side of it.

"Um. Yeah. It's good," he replied. "How's yours?"

She continued as if she hadn't heard his question. "So, I'm just doing some check-ins with everyone." Her mouth began to curl into a smile, but then she broke eye contact to look down at a form on her desk. "You know, your graduation is coming up soon." She paused again, and when Gabe didn't respond, she continued. "So, how is that?"

The question hung shrivelled in the silence between them, like a rotting apple.

"I get that, as your new counsellor, you might not be comfortable talking to me."

Was it appropriate to call her the "new" counsellor? "First" seemed a better fit, given that town hall had only announced the position and hired her in January. Regardless, it was evident that she had little formal training in counselling.

She finally looked away from him and pulled some pamphlets out of her desk drawer. "There are some great, really great, community colleges in the city." She offered him the pamphlets. He saw pictures of men working at construction sites, cutting plywood, looking over blueprints.

"Hmmm?" she said—though it was another malformed question, more noise than word.

He took the pamphlets from her hand with a quiet "thanks," and left.

Classes that day passed quickly and without incident. After school, Gabe worked in the town library, which was actually just an unused corner of the lumber museum with a small table and half-dozen bookcases. Since there was never any work to do in the library, he usually volunteered around the rest of the museum, cleaning glass displays, dusting the ancient furniture and cases. He drew the line at building exhibits, but fortunately the curator, Mrs. Cason, had no interest in updating or changing anything in the museum. It was as though she saw the layout of the building itself as its own, immutable exhibit.

After half an hour of dusting, Gabe's throat was dry and his eyes were sore. Mrs. Cason walked over to him, offering a glass of water.

"Thanks, but I've got my own," he said, grabbing his water bottle from his bag.

"Oh, of course," she replied with a weary chuckle. "You have that thing about tap water." She drank the glass instead.

His gut squirmed as he watched her down all of it. "I just prefer to filter my water first," he muttered.

"Well, I'm sure you know our groundwater is quite clean," she repeated. She had said the same thing every time the topic had come up over the past year of working together. "No need to filter. But it's your choice, of course."

Gabe put his bottle back and left soon after. The nice thing about the small museum was that his shifts were always short. His dislike for Mrs. Cason wasn't helped by the fact that she was also his grade 12 teacher.

The following morning, Gabe arrived at school a few minutes late.

He popped his head into his classroom, trying to determine if he could sneak in without being noticed. Row after row of desks paraded up to a peeling white wood table. Most of them were empty. The students who were there sat silent and focused on the front of the room, where Mrs. Cason was standing.

As Gabe darted into the room, she briefly opened her mouth to speak, then snapped it shut and sat.

Gabe stared at her, and looked around at the rest of the students.

She picked up a permanent marker and pad of paper off her table, then placed them back down and made no further move.

"What's going on?" he asked, the question almost unnecessary.

The two of them paused there like that for fifteen or so seconds, he waiting for her to speak, and she for... well, for whatever she was going to do. He was about to leave and go find whoever else was in the building, when she did something. Mrs. Cason got up again, and adjusted her glasses. And then crumpled to the floor like a fallen piece of paper.

Gabe inhaled sharply without thinking, and gagged on the air. He walked across the room to her body and coughed twice. She'd hit her head. He looked around, but the other students were still silent and looking forward. If their eyes hadn't been open, Gabe would have thought they were asleep.

"Hey!" he yelled at the students.

The girl sitting closest to him, Chelsea, slowly blinked, and unfocused her eyes, then looked down at Gabe and frowned.

"What—?" she began to say, then stopped as she saw Mrs. Cason's face.

Gabe looked back down at her. She was breathing, but her eyes were closed and she wasn't moving. "Do you have a cell phone?" he asked. "Call 911."

As she talked to the operator, Gabe sat back on the floor and pushed against the wall, hauling his legs up to his chest.

When they first moved to the town, Gabe had nightmares most nights of shadowy creatures creeping down from the Ridge and through his bedroom window. No amount of locking the window or covering it with curtains seemed to help, though the nightmares faded in time and were forgotten.

Three years later, when he was 10, Gabe had a single dream about the Ridge. But this wasn't a nightmare, and this vision stayed with him.

He would lie frozen on his bed, head turned and looking out the window at the jumbled, forested hills. The Ridge was high, and looked bigger than in waking life. Dream Gabe recalled learning at the lumber museum that the Ridge was approximately 555 metres tall at its highest peak. It was one of those facts that stayed in his mind, even in dreams.

In this dream, Gabe saw the peak of the Ridge shiver and shake. One enormous blue-black pine caught his attention. He couldn't get up to look closer at it, but instead he felt his eyes somehow focus in on the tree. Soon, he could see each detail clear and distinct. Together, the tree and its smaller neighbours looked like a massive person wearing formal dress. Its sides sloped down from a ruffled tip that resembled a top hat, needle-covered limbs slid out from the trunk gradually at first, like shoulders, then curved down to the ground in sheer droops. From this distance, the sides of the tree flowed like they were smooth and solid. Even Dream Gabe knew that up close, the branches would scratch and tickle and tear, but from his bed it seemed as though the huge tree wore a black midnight gown.

The next morning upon waking up, Gabe wrote everything about the dream down in his notebook. He had to fill in details that he hadn't seen or forgot to remember—the tree had been holding a giant purse, an odd clump of branches that stuck far out into the sky halfway up the trunk. There was the definition of a corset too, wasn't there, hidden away underneath the bulk of needles and wood.

When he peered closer at his memory, Gabe could even see a face: a couple of bare spots near the top of the tree, that cleared an oval of sky coloured in by a silver-grey cloud floating in the background. The face seemed to look out on the centre of town. A silent impenetrable watcher on the Ridge, underneath the bountiful firmament of stars.

It was the stars, by the way, that had woken him up. Gabe couldn't usually see the stars in the skies of Timber Ridge. The night was always too full of dark clouds and rainwater.

The person was a woman, he supposed also, and wrote it down.

Somehow Dream Gabe had forgotten to think of the tree's gender. The omission troubled Waking Gabe for a moment, but then the sun rose and he forgot.

Class was cancelled, of course. As Sandra, one of the two emergency responders in town who did double-duty as first aid and firefighter, took care of Mrs. Cason, Chelsea and the other students packed their bags and left. Gabe was the last to leave. He said nothing to Sandra, but followed his classmates into the hall and outside. Quickly, they dispersed in every direction, like flies swished away by a human hand.

Gabe began the walk home. It was shorter than usual, as he was more awake and less interested in looking around at town. The streets were empty. Either all the cars had woken up and left, or had decided to go back to sleep.

He slowed as he reached the centre of town. The intersection of Cascade and Main was completely still.

He wasn't sure why he was so unsettled by this. Was the town not allowed to be quiet? Were his neighbours not allowed to sleep in?

"What day is it?" he asked himself, almost rhetorically. "How sad is that though, asking yourself a rhetorical question," he retorted in sarcasm.

It was Tuesday. He was pretty sure of that. Any other week, there would have been at least one car driving down the street going somewhere, anywhere. Gabe sighed, and kept walking.

When he got home, the front door was unlocked. As he opened the door, he got a chill and realized all his hairs were standing on end. As usual, all the lights were off. There wasn't enough daylight from the cloud-ridden skies to illuminate the house. But that was okay, because his mom didn't need light. All she needed was her screen and her keyboard and a cup of burnt coffee, watered down by the tap.

He went in the living room and turned on the light, but it was vacant. So was the kitchen, and the spare room downstairs they used for storage. Shivers curdling and pooling at his neck, he ran out and checked the driveway. His mom's Sentra was still there, right where it was when he had seen it coming into the house. Back inside, he checked the bathrooms, but they were all empty. Lastly, he went upstairs. There was only his and his mom's rooms on the second floor, and she was in neither of them.

"Mom!" he yelled. "Where are you?"

As he burst down the stairs, two at a time, he heard the front door open and then slam shut. Gasping and slipping off the last step in surprise, he half-ran, half-stumbled down the hall and around the corner to see his mom, hanging up a coat in the closet.

"What—" she began, then looked at him, eyes and mouth falling wide open.

"Mom," he said, heaving for breath.

She took a step backwards.

"Who are you." It wasn't a question, and he didn't understand it the first time she said it.

"Who are you?" she repeated.

He waited there, finally comprehending her, but unable to even begin formulating a reply.

As he watched, she blinked, tried to refocus her eyes on him again, and then careened into the wall and dropped to the hardwood floor.

Gabe remembered little from the next hour. The phone swinging off the hook as he wiped his tears on a tea towel. Sandra showing up in her converted sedan-turned-ambulance. His mom, gone.

That night, Gabe took his mom's Sentra out for a drive. He grabbed his spiral-bound notebook and drove north out of town, swinging left into the hills along one of the abandoned logging roads. His high-beams did little to aid the trip, as they simply bounced off and through the murk without clearing it. The road switched back and forth on itself, at times winding across fields of thick, bristled stumps and pale sprouts of needle and bark; at others trickling through lost, still verdant growths where the limbs of endless conifers stretched through the sky and blotted out the clouds. His wheels kicked up gravel at every turn as he sped upwards through the patchwork world.

The road continued the corkscrew up the Ridge in increments, ascending into a black, grey, and only occasionally green darkness. Finally, he reached an acceptable clearing. This one was natural—stumpless—and blanketed in stalks of wild wheat. The road by now was faint dirt. If it hadn't been the wet season, Gabe's wheels would have churned up fumes of dust. He stopped the car and looked around out his window. Apart from the ticking down of the engine, the clearing was silent and still. He could see little. The light of the stars did not pervade low enough through the cloud cover to illuminate any but the tips of the stalks. There could have been anything out there. Mice, raccoons, deer. Even a bear.

The clearing should have been cold. Maybe he just didn't notice the temperature. He wandered across the field of stalks. Whenever he stepped on one, it cracked in half with a brittle swish. In the middle of the clearing, he sat down cross-legged, pulled out his notebook and started reading.

There is always something lost in each retelling of a story, he had previously written. *Be it characters smushed to composite or scenes shoved out, by the fifth or fifteenth version little remains of what began. The base is still there, the underlying frame, the fundamental punchline, the things that tugged and tantalized, that kept the story rooted in the reader's long-term memory.*

He paused, hovering the pen tip just above the page, then wrote: *But is that what really matters?*

He paused again, then put the notebook and pen down on the

grass.

Finally, he looked up at the sky. He would have gasped, if there were any gasps left in him to give. The midnight sky was unbounded. He could see no clouds from the clearing, no rain, no storms; nothing but an unfathomable field of bright, watery white-blue grains against the darkest black he had ever seen outside of sleep.

He had missed them, the stars. It felt like years since he had last seen them in their full glory. There was the Little Dipper, spun outwards from the North Star, and there too was Orion's belt. He had never noticed it before, but the other stars in Orion resembled a skirt. He smiled, and laid back against the forest floor.

It really had been years since Gabe had last gazed upon the boundless stars as he was doing so tonight. Ten years, to be exact.

When he was 7, before they moved to Timber Ridge, Gabe's mother threw a dinner party for some friends. While she was downstairs preparing the food, Gabe locked himself in her room and opened the bay window wide. The city's skies brimmed with stardust. He smiled up at them. Then, he got ready. He dragged a short red dress from his mom's closet, and slugged it on. Over his body, it became a beautiful, shimmering floor-length gown. Then he got out a tattered pair of crimson heels, and stepped into them. His feet drowned in the shoes. The heels were low, but still high enough that he had to latch onto walls and door knobs every few steps he took, as he made his way down the hall. Everyone watched as he clomped down the stairs, gripping the railing like a vise. And then, when he had finally reached the main floor, he stood in front of the party, smiled, and curtseyed.

"Who's the little princess?" one of the guests asked, chuckling.

He remembered his mom dragging him by the shoulder up the stairs. He remembered the guests grabbing their coats and rushing out the door. He didn't remember anything more.

And then, he remembered reading one of his old books on star-gazing. Over the years living in Timber Ridge, the books had sat abandoned at the bottom of his bookshelf, but he still recalled a few details from the days when there were stars to see and clear skies to gaze at, and all his books were unread and full of potential. The stars he could see right now were all less than a thousand light-years from the Earth.

All that talk on TV and in movies, when characters repeat the depressing fact that all the stars in the all the skies are dead, that we are just watching their ghosts fade away, that's all fiction. Yes, there are dead stars in the sky, but they can't be seen with the naked eye.

The stars he could see were all there, tantalizing, almost within reach. They were not just echoes.

EMMY MORGAN

Excerpt from the novel
The Ice Princess

In the hallway Monica and Rachel listen before running upstairs. In their shared bedroom Monica closes the door behind her. Rachel runs over to the desktop in the corner and logs onto YouTube.

"We doing this?" Rachel asks with her mouse cursor hovering over the "Upload" button.

Monica looking at the monitor answers, "Do it."

Rachel clicks upload, and there on the worldwide web for the world to see is me dressed in a gold lame gown (portraying Reva Shayne) yelling at Bryant in a wheelchair (portraying Josh Lewis) re-enacting the classic fountain scene from the CBS soap *Guiding Light* in the Andersen backyard from three days ago.

Rachel and Monica found my high school monologue of this very scene (of course I was less Reva more Josh back then... at least physically) on VHS which sparked some sort of interest to film me years later. Oddly enough I went along with it, not knowing they wanted videos for their YouTube channel.

At their computer monitor in their bedroom, Rachel and Monica stare intently at the views.

"Come on." Rachel says trying to will the number up.

"Did you put in enough tags?" Monica asks reaching over the keyboard.

Rachel slaps her hand away. "Yes. Move. Wait wait look."

During the sixty-five minutes Joseph and I are downstairs talking to Ritchard and Kimberly (Alicia is in her trailer with her husband Damian; and Bryant is at soccer practice), the video of Bryant and I labeled "GL's Fountain Scene" gets five-hundred and eight thousand views. They scream and hug each other.

Downstairs we all look up at the ceiling. Ritchard shakes his head; Kimberly rolls her eyes.

I sigh. "To be a teenage girl."

* * *

Over the next few weeks the strangest things begin happening.

First I keep getting these strange emails from SoapCasting.com about wanting to talk to me about working in the soap industry and a phone number. *Bunch of junk*, I think, so of course I delete the email remembering that time I went with Alicia and the kids to a modeling expo and they wanted us to pay for our comp cards. But then four more show up during the week in its place. *Man, spammers are aggressive these days.* I keep pressing delete on the forthcoming emails.

Next up Lynette wants to promote me to Keyholder at Express. I can't believe I'm still here. Working at the same job and my only prospect is full-time Customer Service Rep. The alternative is quit this job and good luck to me finding another job. When I came out they didn't fire me. They changed my name tag in fact, held a meeting telling our store staff about my transition. Lynette (so I'm told) verbally threatened anyone who had a problem with me and stated they would be

from The Ice Princess

fired on the spot, but the thing is if I become a Keyholder aka full-time Customer Service Rep I can stop paying out of pocket for my insurance. No more paying two hundred dollar bills every six months for my follow-ups. Something to think about I suppose.

Third I haven't seen my black family now in over a year. I'm not sad at all. Maybe it's because I have my white family, or maybe I'm just sick of the stress. Although I don't see Alicia as much anymore since she's been married to Damian. I don't have one hundred percent proof but I think he's beating her. I can't get the family riled up without proof.

Speaking of relationships, the final and most odd thing that's occurred is Joseph and I hanging out more and more. Whether we're enjoying a meal at Teapot in Northampton by the Hibachi Grill, sitting under a tree on a full-size AIDS quilt in Boston Common reading *Twilight* together, whale watching on a Hyannisport Ferry Boat, lying on a towel on Hampton Beach under an umbrella, joining me at the soccer game as Monica and Rachel cheer on the squad and clapping for Bryant's goal, or walking hand-in-hand at the Holyoke Mall at Ingleside I find myself longing for his presence on a daily basis. There was one time in my life I was like this... a very long time ago.

Today at the mall he finds a bench in the women's section and sits down while I go into the fitting room carrying clothes on hangers. I end up buying (with my secret credit card Ritchard doesn't know about) a red Valentino butterfly-back silk gown with red Naughty Monkey Candyland pumps, the white Diane von Furstenberg Pansy Ponte di Roma jersey dress I saw in the window, and a pair of Colin Stuart python print peep-toe pumps.

Later that night I walk into my living room, sits down on my couch, and cozy up next to him. It was in that very moment on my couch after all these months I realized out loud.

"I haven't met your folks."

He turns his head towards me. "What?"

"You know damn well you heard me." I say sitting up. "I haven't met your folks. We've been consumed with my family and my life. Not once have I met your family."

He begins to stumble.

"Are you ashamed of me?" I ask.

"No no baby it's not that." He says taking my hand with his free hand as he moves the hand that was holding my shoulders to rub my arm. "I'm proud to be your…boyfriend? I'm your boyfriend right? Cuz we never technically had that discussion."

"Yes you are. Don't try to change the subject." I brush his hand away from my arm and fold both my arms over my chest. "You know…" I want to tell him about Marcus and my past with him. But how do I do that? It's been months. *Maybe I should leave well enough alone.* The words don't leave my mouth. I lower my head and he runs his hands on the side of my face. He pulls me into a warm, apologetic kiss. It ends up being more than just a kiss.

I fix my hair in the bathroom mirror before adjusting my boobs in the Victoria's Secret black lace teddy I bought secretly while he was in Radio Shack. I flick the light switch off and see Joseph asleep in my bed. I giggle thinking about how this is like that scene in "Pretty Woman." I walk over to him and sit on the edge of the bed.

"He sleeps." I say with a smile before kissing him on the lips. Unlike the movie Joseph stays asleep, I turn off the lamp on his side of the bed, and walk around to climb into the other side.

When he senses me in bed, he rolls over, putting his arm over my stomach. He kisses my temple before we both enter sleepland.

Sitting at a wedding reception at the Delaney House in Holyoke, I tug up my tangerine strapless sheath dress. Then I notice a piece of lettuce on Joseph's lapel. I pick it off and smooth a hand down his grey pinstriped suit. Without stopping to eat his Waldorf salad he nods a thank you. Two female guests gush over my shoes, but I'm completely oblivious. The new Lynette Coleman dressed in her wedding gown

from The Ice Princess

comes over to hug me. Lynette shoos the shoe gawkers away. Her new husband Montgomery "Monty" shakes Joseph's hand.

The window fan blows in the morning air while Joseph lies shirtless and awake on his back in my queen sized bed. I'm next to him snuggled into that body nook with his arm around me. He smiles while watching me still asleep.

As I awaken, I look up at his face and am startled. "What are you doing?"

"Just watching you sleep." He whispers kissing my forehead. "Hey we should get to work soon. I am gonna go fix us breakfast."

"You don't know my kitchen." I challenge him.

He kisses my forehead again. "I will find my way." I lift up enough to let his arm free; he jumps out of bed and rushes to the kitchen.

I reach over to my night stand and grab my cell phone. I take the charging cable out and start dialing.

Alicia picks up on the other end. "What's up, Dee?" On the other end of the line she walks around her store.

"How'd you know it was me?" I ask.

"All cell phones have caller ID." She holds the phone away and shakes her head before bringing it back to her ear. "I'm the natural blond remember? So what happened?"

I begin to whisper before getting up to close my bedroom door a crack. "Joseph is making breakfast for us."

"Did you two-" Alicia starts.

"No. I don't think we are ready for that." I say as I climb back in bed.

"So what happened?" Alicia probes. "Did you two fool around?"

"Actually we haven't. He either falls asleep or I'm just not in the mood. Maybe I bore him."

"That is so cute." Alicia says as she rings a customer up balancing the cordless on her shoulder. "Well I don't wanna play the devil's advocate, but I do think it's sweet that you two are together and all. I had no idea you two met in college, and now this. You couldn't write that stuff."

"I know, but it's moving too fast." Desiré says. "I feel the same way as you do about the whole situation, but at the same time I want things to go slow. Leesh, he knows me. What and who I am, and he accepts me for that. He makes me feel so good about myself, and well that scares the shit outta me. And don't say I can't live in the past. I know I am still not fully over the rape, my bio family, and all the other shit that went on in my life even before all this. I just want a second to be alone and sit in my problems ya know?"

Joseph comes down the hall balancing a tray of breakfast food, but stops when he hears me talking on the phone.

Alicia continues, "I think he is a nice guy, but I don't know. My only thing, Dee, is knowing he's Marcus' brother after what Marcus did. I won't say anything to him; that's just weird. I wonder if Marcus said anything to him." A brief silence gives Alicia time to do what she's good at: making a tense situation funny. "I know he's white and all but what if he's got a lead pipe in his pants."

"Jesus don't say that. Hey what if he is hung like a Tic-Tac?"

"Nah I heard he's big actually. He may rip you a new one."

The silence is deafening. Alicia tries to recover, "Oh my god, I didn't mean that."

"It's okay." I assure her. "I mean funny thing is I realize I was raped, but I don't feel like I was anymore. I don't feel that monster inside my body anymore; at this point I'm just dealing with the emotions of it. Ten points for the pun though."

"That was good huh?" Alicia chuckles to herself, but then stops herself. "Totally un-pc but good."

"You don't have a politically correct bone in your body." I say. "Meanwhile I'd settle for any bone at this point." Then I hear the floor creak. "Joseph is coming back I should go. Talk to you later."

"Bye honey. I love you." Alicia says.

from The Ice Princess

"Love you too."

As we hang up, I turn to see Joseph coming in the bedroom with a tray of food: sizzling bacon, four French toast triangles, six perfectly flat pancakes, two glasses of Orange Juice, a plate full of scrambled eggs, and a bowl of homefries.

"Thank you, babe." I say as I lean over the tray to kiss him.

He puts the tray on the bed in front of me, climbs in bed next to me, and begins eating the food with me. He turns on my VCR remote as we watch *It Happened One Night*.

* * *

Joseph holds open the entrance door to the Enfield Mall as I rush in past him. We barrel past the four elderly people dressed in identical light blue sweat suits who are speed walking. A young mother rocks a baby carriage back and forth as she stares into the front of the J. Crew window while drinking a coffee in a Starbucks plastic cup. Two older Asian men with "Maintenance" name tags assist each other changing the garbage bags of a trash can. I maneuver past Charlton, the overweight Middle Eastern Mall Security Cop, on his Segway with Joseph behind me. Just in front of Structure, Joseph pulls me back by the arm.

"Dee, I am gonna go to work; I will see you in a bit, ok?" He lightly kisses me. "Listen, take it easy. You're just a few minutes late, okay?" He holds me till I calm down.

I take a deep breath, plaster a smile across my face, peck kiss him back, and sneak past the customers into the back room.

Joseph walks briskly in the opposite direction of me adjusting his "Pagano's" apron. He scurries behind the counter into the kitchen. As he rushes past, an older version of himself closes the kitchen doors behind him. His father pushes Joseph back into the wall. Joseph glares at him with all the rage in his body. Suddenly Joseph charges at him clamping his hands around his father's neck. His father's head knocks down all the pots and pans hanging from the ceiling. Outside the kitchen patrons perk up at the sound of the brawl destroying the kitchen. Marcus claps his hands to the two waitresses and a cook who stand paralyzed staring at the closed kitchen door. Mrs. Pagano moves to the kitchen door, but Marcus stands in front of her.

"They need to do this." He says as he walks Mrs. Pagano back to the front of the pizza shop.

They decide in silence to ignore the commotion and carry on business as usual.

In the Structure back room, Krissy dressed in denim cut offs with a plaid purple short-sleeved button down walks in. She pulls her bone straight jet black hair in a low ponytail while she walks to the office I'm in. The sound of her Chuck Taylor Converse sneakers scuffing the floor alerts me of her presence.

"Hey Dee." Krissy chirps.

I look up at her from the mountain of paperwork. I am about to say hi back, but despite her chipper greeting I notice a worried look on her face. "What is it, Krissy?"

Walking as fast as my legs can carry me without running, I finally make it to the front of Pagano's. Just as I am about to walk in, Marcus moves in front of me and ushers me to the side.

"Listen, now is not a good time." He whispers still holding onto my arm.

My eyes focus on his hand but slowly and eventually stare him back in the eyes. I can't read them like before. He must have noticed he was still gripping my arm because he let go.

"Oh, I'm sure you're just concerned for your brother." I finally muster.

Joseph's battered presence behind Marcus shifts my eyes away. Marcus follows my eyes, turns around, and sees Joseph. Without a word, Marcus leaves.

I move towards Joseph and gingerly touch his bruised eye. His head recoils in pain as he also takes a step back.

A step I immediately notice. "Oh, I see," I flatly stated.

"I'm so sorry…" He starts but the tears choke the rest of his words preventing him from finishing any explanation.

Standing in front of Joseph, I suddenly turn and walk away leaving him alone and bruised. As I slowly carry myself on my legs down the hall back to Structure I see a couple. The tall blond Caucasian boyfriend stands next to his short blond Caucasian girlfriend with his hand on her back as they look at sunglasses at a kiosk. *They look like what Ken and Barbie would look like if they were human.* The girlfriend tries on a crazy pair of sunglasses and turns to her boyfriend. They laugh as she checks herself in the mirror. I stop dead in my tracks for a moment to stand and watch them. *When do I get my love story? My happy ending? Why does everything have to be so fucking complicated? I deserve what those two have. Why is it so fucking hard?* I shove the rest of my thoughts down and meander towards Structure unaware the couple has walked ahead of me and is inside the store.

As I walk in my zombie state, I walk behind the cash wrap. Steven, dressed in a slate blue button down with rolled up sleeves and dark jeans, is ringing up the same couple I saw at the kiosk. At first I don't notice them as I'm busy going over hourly numbers, but then I get the feeling I'm being stared at; I look up from the binder. The couple stares at me. *How'd they get so far ahead of me that they selected and purchased something? How long was I standing there?*

Krissy comes up beside me and whispers, "You okay, sweetie?" Krissy takes the untagged items and heads back to the customer putting it in a shopping bag before smiling at them as they leave.

"Yeah." I respond.

Steven hands the boyfriend his receipt; then he walks the couple to the front of the store. "And I'm Steven."

Steven shakes both of their hands. "Thanks for stopping at Structure. Come back anytime."

As the couple walks past the Structure display window the boyfriend looks back at me. "Have a good one."

I instantly snap back into retail manager mode, "Thanks, sir, you too." I even add a wave.

Starting to walk out of my sight, I see the girlfriend nudge her boyfriend. At that moment something clicks, and I see the boyfriend's face as clear as day. It morphs from his smile at her now to his same smile as he danced with me at a club. *That's the guy from the club I danced with. He dragged me onstage and got pissed I left him.* I snap out of my trance and run from behind the counter to the front of the store. Standing in the middle of the mall with my hands on my head in both directions I no longer see the couple. *Could he have been the one that raped me? No it was Sloane. I know that.* I think to myself. Then I remember the reason I didn't want to finish dancing with him. In my head I hear the remix of "Alone" by Heart.

I walk back inside Structure defeated. I notice a tall blond slightly overweight man dressed in an EMT uniform sifting through the piles of jeans stacked along the wall near the dressing rooms. Using work as my distraction I approach him.

Like a robot I instruct him about proper size and fit. He's smiling, and then I realize he's blushing. After taking a few outfits to his dressing room, I walk to the cash wrap. He follows coming out of the dressing room with some jeans and t-shirts in hand. Reaching over the counter to take the items from him, I begin my Structure credit card sales pitch. He interrupts my usual spiel with his agreement to sign up.

I detach the bottom portion of the price tags on his purchase items, fold them into a neat pile on the counter behind the cash wrap, and move to the end register. "There are a couple questions I need to ask. First what is your name, sir?"

"Shayne Gomes." He says sliding down to the end register to her.

from The Ice Princess

"I know pale as a ghost. My dad's Brazilian; mom's Cuban." He rolls his eyes at himself. "What else you need?" He asks clearing his throat.

I punch keys on the cash register while looking at the monitor. "Last four of your social, please?"

"8267." He says quietly while leaning over the counter.

I punch more keys. "House or apartment number?"

"76." He says as he skims at the credit card brochure I put on the counter.

"Zip code?" I ask.

"01108." He is much more involved in the brochure now.

"And your phone number?" I ask as I finally look up.

"Is that for you or the computer?" He asks just as I see his skin go flush again.

I smile uncomfortably. "The computer." I look back down at the monitor.

"860-555-3344." He says while closing his eyes to remember.

"Ok." I finish and move from the register back to his purchases putting them in a shopping bag. "I am gonna start ringing you up while your credit check processes."

I scan the bottom portion of the price tags into the register one register down. The end register finally processes a receipt. I grab it, scan the barcode from the receipt to complete the transaction in the register. I hand Shayne the bag as the approval slip prints out. After he signs the receipt, I grab the pen along with a temporary credit card from the other register.

I write information on the temporary credit card pamphlet not looking up at him. "Ok, you were approved for a $1,500 limit. And like I mentioned, I took ten percent off this purchase today." I hand him the temporary credit card then take the signed approval slip from him.

"Cool. Thanks." Shayne places the pen on the counter. "Now I guess you will be seeing more of me." He again rolls his eyes at himself.

I smile as I place the approval slip in a drawer near the cash register. I notice the extra printout from the credit card approval at the end register, and hand it to him.

"Don't forget this. It has your phone number on it." I inform him.

"You keep it." He smiles at me before he leaves.

Yeah no. I wait till he leaves the store before throwing it in the waste basket under the register.

BOOK TWO

PREFACE TO
THE ORIGINAL ANTHOLOGY

Is it even possible to speak of fiction by trans women of color in 2015? Of the handful of our novels and short stories in existence much of it is self-published work and, as a result, has received almost no critical attention, almost no readership. And yet we are told that trans women of color are part of a thriving movement of transgender literature – that our time has come. But when we so much as glance at the opportunities in literary work and publishing that our white trans sisters have had access to, it's obvious that there's a great divide between us. Because, while they have new novels published, new short stories added to anthologies, new credits writing for film and television, new interactive fiction and games every year, our impact amounts to barely a fraction of published trans fiction.

In fact, our entire body of fiction consists almost entirely of the work of a few individual trans women of color who have enjoyed exceptional opportunities. We do not call this success, however, because we see that it is only ever a few of us who are allowed a voice at any given time. We understand well that when only some of us are allowed to publish or otherwise receive support or payment for our creative work, it is not genuine opportunity but rather the curse of tokenism. The curse takes one of two paths: 1) you're damned if you let them make you an exception (your work will be constrained, it will never be your own but always symbolic of your identities/communities, you will be dehumanized and treated not as a person but as an idea) or 2) you're damned if you don't let them (your work will be shut out, exploitation pays a pittance but nonconformity means you get nothing, your art ends here before it begins).

If it isn't apparent already, what we're describing is a condition of permanent crisis. Just as black trans women and other trans women of color are being murdered with impunity in devastating numbers, just as the value of our lives means essentially nothing to our communities of color and to our supposed white trans allies and the legal authorities who kill us through their own brands of violence and forced marginalization, so also are our voices, our innovations, and our collective memory made worth nothing.

And yet because we are trans women of color, because we have survived this condition of permanent crisis, living at various intersections of oppression, our voices are all the more important. The stories in this book serve as indisputable evidence of the strength, perceptiveness, boldness, creativity, political consciousness, and unapologetic capacity for openness and truth-telling of trans women of color.

The stories in this anthology confront major themes and issues in the lives of trans women of color with profound honesty and attention toward helping one another heal. A story like "The Girl and the Apple," by Jasmine Kabale Moore, not only unflinchingly describes the sense of ever-present danger that many of us feel in public spaces (including the hyper-vigilant condition of trauma that results from repeated exposure to intense scrutiny and violence) it also provides invaluable emotional support to other trans women of color by accurately reflecting, and therefore validating, our experiences and our perceptions of reality.

Preface to the Original Anthology

A number of other stories explore their own kinds of traumas and begin to show us a way to survive them, a day at a time. In contrast, there are also stories in our anthology that take up a completely different subject matter – genre fantasies, memories and the past, self-acceptance, relationships with family and friends, romance and intimacy, and language itself – but they do so in the specific context of our lives as trans women of color.

While this anthology serves as one of the first examples of representation of trans women of color's fiction, we would be committing an injustice to trans women of color everywhere to claim this anthology as a definitive and comprehensive text of our works. The stories of many trans women are missing from this collection, not for lack of their existence or for lack of ability on our part as writers, but rather due to the lack of resources and reach of this anthology. The stories of undocumented and incarcerated trans women, sex workers, Indigenous, Asian, and black trans women among others are still not represented as they deserve to be. As such, this anthology should serve as a point of revival of writing among trans women of color, trans feminine people of color, and nonbinary amab people of color. We hope that through the writing set forth in this compilation, we inspire others to actualize the trans writing movement we have been promised. With this work, we look forward to a future where our stories, factual and fictional are valued and shared.

Jamie Berrout & Ellyn Peña

JASMINE KABALE MOORE
The Girl and the Apple

Marjorie now spoke to herself in a voice that echoed sovereignty, but was not.

"There is a swelling in your throat that forbids you to look at the sun - or at God. This is why religion has proven to be difficult for you. You refuse to face each other honestly. You have been looking in the face of ill intent so long, it has grown tired of your friendship and he's turned his head to others to turn their eyes at your throat. And you stand huddled with yourself for the ground leaves you to your devices. Paranoia is truth. They want to kill you. They would if they knew. They will hurt you. They will have a reason to harm you if you look to God. There will be no Providence. The lump in your neck chokes you and it knocks like a ritual. Your mother's family must have had worship before missionaries. Did they have Gods? Witchcraft? A stew that would slide the device down as you swallow? It was magic that spirited you to womanhood. But there's no magic to call to now. You're an observer to yourself."

"Hey sister!"

Marjorie lifted her head to find an older black man – maybe in his mid 50s – he had a military green coat zipped to the very top covering his salt and pepper chin and jawline. Black sweat pants that billowed and pressed against his thin calves when the wind called for it.

"Hey sister. You got some change?"

As she reached for her wallet, her fingers brushed against the book she was rereading, "Their Eyes Were Watching God" by Zora Neale Hurston. She had a habit of throwing whatever book stood around her room into her bag before she went anywhere. The quote "Real Gods require blood" rang and ricocheted across her mind. Silently, she dropped all of her change into the man's hand, amounting to 3 quarters, 5 nickels, and a penny.

"Thank you sister. You have a blessed day."

After he was out of sight she went inside the train station and walked across a great hall to catch the 10:45 train to Cleveland. While in the waiting area, she was forced to stand because all of the seats were filled and no one seemed to want to get up for her. She leaned against a ticket desk. Never was she a sound sleeper and premature exhaustion from her emanating journey weighed heavy.

"Don't fall asleep in public," Marjorie thought to herself. "When you are alone, people will take from you. Attach your belongings to your person. Your body may not think your objects hold value when you're visited by your past lives."

The glass doors of the boarding docks were opened and wedged, letting in a gust that stirred the pigeons that had huddled inside for the warmth to take flight.

Marjorie furtively handed her ticket for the 10:45 to the clerk; she put on her brightest smile in hopes to distract him from her birth name printed in big black letters across the top of it. He frowned at her and the blood retreated from his face. It didn't go unnoticed. She reacted by darting her eyes for the nearest exit and calculated how many people she would have to shove to get there. Marjorie then eyed his chest for a name tag. His name was Jason. Jason was now scanning Marjorie's body for signs. His eyes stopped at her chest, between her legs, her feet. He worked his way back up to her hands, her throat. Jason asked to see her identification. He studied it dubiously, comparing her choppy straight hair in the photo to her shroud of curly black hair that kept falling in her face. But her dark eyes and the smile directed at him were the same. Marjorie could hear the family behind her getting restless. The zippers opening and closing and suitcases shifting from hand to hand. The other clerk at the desk was now looking at Jason questioningly.

"What's the hold up?"

"Nothing," replied Jason.

He quickly jabbed Marjorie's ticket and ID into her hand.

"Thank you. Go straight and to the left to find your train, ma'am er sir."

She heard a whispered "What?" come from behind her. Without replacing her returned objects into her bag, she lifted her knit black scarf over her chin and entered the boarding dock in a practiced rush that resembled being busy and having better places to be but was not. Her whole body was fevered and thus dewy under her scarf. She fanned herself with her ticket to the confusion of an attendant (it was 44 degrees), who was in front of her train directing passengers to their seats. The same attendant pulled her suitcase on board before helping her inside with a precariously placed footstool. Her seat was 285C and her designation row was empty.

"Ah a window."

She exhaled and took her seat. After about 15 minutes on the motionless train, her mind started to wander.

"Don't fall asleep in public," she thought to herself. "You have been told you talk in your sleep. Your body may betray you and your voice coaching when you're speaking to your abusers. Who could hear you when you're pleading for help in a dream? The waking world listens to your intonation but only because they think you're an octave too low."

The seat 285C shifted and rose slightly.

"Hello."

Marjorie mourned her otherwise peaceful train ride. The woman who sat beside her had black square glasses, a light brown bob, and a smile that further rounded out her face.

"Hi." Marjorie attempted to simultaneously sound as warm as she could while conveying how boring she was.

"Where are you headed?"

"Cleveland, you?"

"Cleveland. I was just in DC to speak at a law conference."

Marjorie replied with what she thought was a conversation ending, "Hm."

Discreetly checking her hair and face in the faded reflection of the window to make sure she still looked effortless and cisgender (although she made sure she had three hours to do her make-up, hair, and wardrobe), she noted her leather jacket could come off and that she needed another coat of lip gloss. In her compact, as she was reapplying her mouth, she spotted black moles on her neck that were not there before. Her neck and wrists were adorned with the decomposition flakes of her beloved jacket. She peeled away the archipelagic faux leather freckles from her skin and thought of the things she'd have to give up to purchase another jacket. The train lunged forward and with that solidified that she was really leaving DC. Going to Cleveland didn't seem real to her before, even with the extensive planning, until train 538 hurdled itself west.

"I'm from Cleveland actually," chimed the passenger next to her.

"Yeah?"

"Is this your first time going?"

"No. I've been a few times."

"Have you ever been to the farmers market there?"

"No. Never heard of it."

The Girl and the Apple

"Really? It's a big occasion. It's hard to believe you wouldn't have ran into it."

Marjorie thought of her and her best friend Cassandra walking home from the hole in the wall bar that Cassandra's mother worked at down the street from her home, on a wet summer night and heels clicking on cobblestone. That night Marjorie found Cassandra crying on the steps of the not so curiously placed church across the street from the bar. Her mother's abusive boyfriend Matt had shown up and demanded a portion of the tips she had accumulated. Marjorie called her own mother the next day to remind her that she wished to receive a name from her. To tell her mother that her ID would go unchanged until she named her. About how awkward and unsettling it was to present her capital "M" for MALE to the faces of gatekeepers. What Marjorie didn't tell her was how she felt dejected and left behind when she was not included in the collective phrase "the girls" when she referred to her daughters. How she second-guesses every decision minor and major alike because she has been told that what she felt was true to her would be a harbinger of mutilation and pernicious alienation.

"I don't understand, I've given you a name already," Mom said. "You're a boy. I pushed you out of me. I put baby boy clothes on you. I changed your diapers."

Something tethered Marjorie's mouth shut then. She didn't know quite what it was, but she presumed it was guilt. Guilt that transitioning has caused her family suffering. Guilt for the childhood photos she burned. It was the apple in her throat. It strangled her.

"Tell me about the farmers market there. I'd love to go with my friend," Marjorie said to the passenger. Her anxiety now subsiding, she felt guilt for how rude she'd been before.

"Oh, well it's on the west end of the city. It's been there as far as I can recall. So you can imagine how old it is." She chuckled lightly. Marjorie smiled and looked at the passenger's hands.

"I'm Victoria by the way. What's your name?"

"Marjorie."

"Nice to meet you Marjorie."

Victoria reached for Marjorie's hand and gently rubbed the pad of her thumb against her forefinger's base knuckle.

"It was built over a hundred years ago. There's a high clock tower above the shops," Victoria mused. "You really can't miss it unless you were coming from Lorain. And inside! The ceiling must be at least 40 feet high. The intermittent skylights look like cream, whipped concave into the yellow brick. I went often when I was a girl. The breads from the bakeries there are unmatched. We went every other Saturday when the weather permi-" The passenger's phone rang loudly in her purse. "I'm sorry." She said as she answered her phone in Spanish. Marjorie took this opportunity to traipse to the restroom.

She felt like an acrobat on a shaky ribbed tightrope. A grip of beige varying sized dots dispersed sparingly over royal blue wool on the aisle seats served as a balancing tool. Other passengers retracted their limbs as to not cast her down. The hall of plastic door restrooms on the low level of the train was empty. There were seven of them, three on either side and one at the very end of the hall with a blue plaque contrasted by a white figure sitting in a wheelchair. Two of the plastic doors had not been latched properly so they swung against the other doors with every rattle the train gave. She examined the restrooms for characters with dresses or shirts but found nothing. The air smelled sour inside the restroom she chose. Like an expired botanical perfume found in a clearance bin. She placed her dark peach concealer on the rim of the sink and looked for excavated areas on her face, worn by weather and time. There was a portent black islet on her collarbone she had missed. She had that jacket before she had her chosen name. It was there the day she bought it from the mall she worked at. She was subsequently followed home on foot by a gremlin of a man that was known around her neighborhood to stalk and proposition young black women for sex. It was there not an hour ago when Jason was inspecting her like a farmer does cattle. Conceding to the amusing notion that she felt like an imitator in an imitation leather garment; she made a note in her phone to look into veganism.

When Marjorie returned, the passenger was watching detritus slip past the aisle. By some legerdemain, when Marjorie took her seat, they dug into a tunnel.

"Trains are capricious vehicles."

"It's easier to walk on shells."

"A good friend of mine just called me, she reminded me of the last time we went to the market when we were in junior high. Alice took me a few days after my grandma passed away to get blue fleshed potatoes at a Peruvian shop there."

"Blue?"

"They grow along hillsides on the island of Amantani in Lake Titicaca. My grandma made mashed potatoes with a blue hue when I was young. I remember it tasted like sweet cream so it was the only way I would eat them."

Marjorie's anti-androgen pills had the intended effect of being a potassium-sparing diuretic. They inhibit testosterone at nascence; but in addition to making her skin softer it raised her potassium level to highs that made eating foods enriched with it treacherous. Eating potatoes of any value could potentially cause her hyperkalemia.

"I don't remember waking up that morning. I spent the entire day shaking myself from a dream. The market felt like a vigil. Standing under the clock tower somehow made me..."

Victoria was looking at the covers of travel pamphlets through a shiny mesh pocket attached to the seat in front of her for the word. "Atavistic. The four faces availed to the endless directions of my solar system. I could discover the start of everything from the spire of that century-standing clock tower. I wanted to run my fingers through the pools of time."

Sunshine sloped into the train in decks, instantly making the cushions of their seats feel softer. Exiting the tunnel; an incantation for the floor under their feet to grow lush.

Victoria continued. "I was dipped in reverie. My limbs brushed my body softly as I entered the concourse. I slipped across walls, leaving trails of dust. Every person I was pressed against no matter how briefly, I spoke to in a silent language. There were flower shops inside. Larkspur the same dizzying azure as my favorite supper meal. Bound together and falling at me. The odds of a vegetable and a flower blossom growing the same hue awed me. It's quite a common color on this planet but the image of something that bright being harvested in soil dyed the folds of my brain. This shade of blue should be written about on the wall of a cave somewhere. In some archaic language that will bring you dreams of premonitions upon reading it aloud. Carved into flotsam of an ancient drowned ship. Washed, floating on a tide above schools of fish and miles of ocean."

Marjorie got the feeling that she was missing orbs of worlds fly past as she listened to Victoria. The rays of an alien sun ebbed into the stale air in their craft. It was so lovely to be in this corner. In the nuance that lives in the little places. The places on the planet that transmuted conditions by the nature of their existence. Victoria draped across her right, closing to the thoroughfare. Blinding as the window adjacent. She didn't want to miss anything else or flex Victoria out of her daydream by speaking.

"I wish I could trace the origin lines of that color to the primordial. Somehow write my name on the line between. I wish to know every great coincidence. Ineluctable accidents. Ephemeral because they live."

"I think we may be a coincidence." Marjorie couldn't stop herself from being honest. "I sometimes feel I can't wake up. I am consistently absconding. And I atone for my elusory conduction. Every space I'm in is a source of consternation."

"When I was younger, I was frightened by everything. It was maddening to me to be seen. It was impossible to navigate the world because I couldn't see myself in it."

"Has that changed?"

"Late in my transition I started calibrating where in the world I could fit. Years after I started being regarded as a woman, I could see the space I occupy as valid. Only then could I relax into the breadth of my community."

Marjorie wondered why Victoria decided to disclose. Had she been spotted by Victoria? Does Victoria see her? Had her words given her away? Her voice? Marjorie folded in on herself. Her arms in the pockets of her torso. She became small in a small corner.

HELLO PASSENGERS THIS IS YOUR CONDUCTOR SPEAKING. THANK YOU FOR CHOOSING US AS YOUR TRAVEL COMPANION. TO ALL PASSENGERS JUST BOARDING, SOMEONE WILL COME BY TO COLLECT YOUR TICKETS SO PLEASE HAVE THEM READY. WE WILL BE STOPPING AT HARPERS FERRY SHORTLY. FEEL FREE TO USE THE DINING CAR FOR REFRESHMENTS. THANK YOU AGAIN FOR CHOOSING US.

"Do you want to join me? I skipped breakfast."

"Oh no. I just have some reading I want to do."

"Okay well I'll be down there if you want to find me."

"It was nice meeting you."

When Victoria stood, she projected the side of her jaw up and above Marjorie. She cast her eyes from a lifted angle as if to get an adversarial view. She whisked away to her forage.

Marjorie half drew the window curtain. Concealed from her reflection she could observe the listless barnyards. Another train rocked past as they dropped under a bridge. She couldn't imagine herself telling anyone she was transgender if she were as far into her transition as Victoria was. There would be no foreseeable reason. No one should know. Unnerved and alone she opened "Their Eyes were Watching God".

Janie was on her third husband when a man took the passengers seat, opened his legs at an incomprehensible angle, tilted his hat over his eyes and almost instantly started snoring and muttering in his sleep.

"A couple more hours," she said to herself.

The train slinked further, advancing into twilight at a knowing pace. All of the passengers were now surrounded by a large field with a single oak tree that watched over the grass, ambivalent to them. For a moment a blue light covered all things. To the left about a quarter mile away was a police car pulling someone over. To her right stood an outline of a man. He seemed to be focused on her. The train was now dim and she had to wait for her eyes to adjust to see that he was wearing a uniform. He was an attendant.

"Hey." He said. "You want a seat to yourself?"

Marjorie was eager for space for her long legs.

"Yes, please."

She took hold of her bag and followed the attendant down the aisle. The other passengers looked at her and she pitied them for having to share seats with strangers. A few carriages later, the attendant stopped and extended his arm presenting her to her new isolated row.

"Here you go, I'm Tristan by the way. What's your name Miss?" He was smiling and Marjorie envied how rested into his gender he appeared to be.

"I'm Marjorie. Thank you for this, maybe I can get some sleep now."

"Yeah no problem, I'll be back in a bit to check on you."

"Awe, thank you again."

Tristan nodded at her and between the bucking of the train and the empty overhead storage bars that shadowed his face, it looked like he was bouncing his head against them as he did, letting out a deep cough that curtailed into a growl at the final bar.

Marjorie settled into her new space. This rail car was unoccupied and warm. The windows seemed clearer in moonlight. She sent Cassandra a text to tell her she would arrive shortly so be sure to make her way to the station. She had met Cassandra on Myspace when they were both 16 and had different names than their present ones. Later, when it became plain she had to answer to something that wasn't classically male, she placed the responsibility of surrogacy into Cassandra's hands. She would use her birth name until her parents embraced her as a third daughter. She was exercised in the ways of magnanimity when it came to her mother.

Marjorie had returned home from a sleep over one Sunday with painted nails and pierced ears. Her mother looked repulsed. The femininity made her nauseous.

"You may look like a girl but you will never be one." She said, enthusiastic with her own derision. "Why can't you just be a gay guy? You make people uncomfortable with the way you look. It's weird."

"But I'm not a gay guy, mom. I'm a girl." Marjorie confessed this and felt ashamed with her own existence. She realized this must have sounded grotesque to her mother.

"How? What did I do to you to deserve this?"

"This isn't about you. I'm more comfortable this way."

"What about your family?"

They would have this same argument for years. Passion would billow into it when they had to be at any public place at the same time. Marjorie would replay this scene in her head every time she had to show documentation. It was self-abasement whenever she left the house. So she reveled in her lonesome carriage that flung her across depth-less lakes and burrowed her into tunnels. Through dense verdure and above spurned warehouses, the carriage enveloped and cradled her into a dream. She dreamed she was sitting in the bower of that oak tree covered by a basin blue light. Zora Neale Hurston sat across from her on the ground, her hair was cropped and curled to the bottom of her split earlobes. Earrings had been pulled from her body.

"My jewelry was the color of that tree." She spoke directly and clearly. She said, "I was missing something when I gave birth to you. That's why you've never loved anyone. You don't even love me."

When Marjorie woke, it was dark. She was staring at her palm out of her only open eye. Her tongue felt like it needed to be wrung out and she wondered if someone laid clay in her mouth. There was something sucking the wet from her, dispensing it and forming a beginning. There was clay coating her throat and accumulating at an unknown stop. She hadn't had anything to drink for hours and she needed to rinse her throat. When she stood to rush for the dining car, her vision went black. She hadn't eaten either, she thought of Zora's ears. Heat flashed, spread, and centered to the top of her scalp. She felt swollen with a burning rising under her skin, a burning that was impregnated by dread. She was frightened by everything moving so quickly. By the howl tearing through the tracks. By the sound of a person directly behind the door of her car collecting mucus at the back of their maw and expectorating. Her vision cleared and her jacket appeared igneous with the promise of new Hell. She began to pray. "I'm scared. I'm scared. I'm scared. I'm frightened. Someone give me courage. Please give me bravery." She focused on the word bravery for a moment. Praying the word into herself. An automatic sliding door opened in earshot, coinciding with a hacking spit. Marjorie made out the figure down the aisle holding a container to be Tristan. She couldn't see his face but the sound of his comfortable masculinity was clue enough. A text from Cassandra that read, "Omg bitch!!! You're almost here! Ahhh!!!!" lit the inside of her open bag,

The Girl and the Apple

illuminating her wallet.

"What time does the dining car close?" asked Marjorie. She placed her hand across her clavicle as though she could cover the dry inside.

"Soon Miss. You'll miss it if you don't hurry. I came to see about you."

"Really? Thank you. I'm fine, I'm just going to get some water."

"I'll follow you."

"You don't have to."

"I'll show you where it is."

"I'll find it."

Tristan couched his cup of saliva between two seats.

"I want to know what you do."

"Excuse me?"

"Where do you work?"

"Oh retail. I'm sorry but I'll die if I don't get some water in me."

Marjorie felt the backhand of isolation twist her face around to look for witnesses, no one.

"Sure," he said. And he side-stepped over to his spittoon.

Marjorie twisted her hair into a bun while she walked to the door.

"Would you ever dominate a white man?"

She palmed her pepper spray in her bag and studied his face for the first time. He was shorter than she was and he had a hat on, masking his eyes to her completely. The apples of his cheeks were flat but his florid face was wide with sagging jowls. His teeth were sharp and lined with a colonnade of saliva in his open smiling mouth.

"No."

He laughed from the same place he growled and extended his arm towards the sliding door.

Entering the next carriage full of sleeping passengers, she felt her panic fires dim and extinguish. What replaced her terror was shame.

Humiliation in her unrest from alienation. What if instead of transitioning she took heed to her fathers adjuration? In his most pleasant voice, "Don't change. Can you do this for me?" when he drove her to the pride clinic in Baltimore. Instead of navigating endless streams of trains anonymously; she would be welcomed into the clay tide of Lake Titicaca with waves that don't break but mold downwards. She would hold the crescent undisturbed until an undulating reed boat drew a trail over her drowned body.

She drafted a text to Cassandra on her procession to the next car.

"Ugh there's this creepy guy here that won't leave me alone."

Her bag knocked on the head of a sleeping passenger who then stirred in their place. She began to form a whisper of compunction but halted when Cassandra texted back.

"We'll get you a knife girl."

Marjorie imagined breaking the strands of liquid strung over Tristan's teeth with a switchblade.

Water was two carts down so she pulled her gift card out of her wallet. Her older sister, Angelina, gave Marjorie a card with 100 dollars on it for Christmas, not wanting to buy her a wrongly sexed item. When she was inspecting the card for a CID number to finalize her train ticket purchase online, she noticed that it brandished no name of ownership. Committed to being patient with her mothers renaming she transferred all of her funds to the provisional gift card where she could remain unknown. Everything she owned was bought by a nameless woman.

A staircase that descended into the dining level offered itself to her right. There were six plum booths and a woman sitting in the nearest one. In line, there was a man taking his receipt for a chocolate bar and another man queued behind him. Upon Marjorie's arrival, she caught the woman's eye. It was Victoria and she was waving languidly at her. There were no windows on the lower level. There

The Girl and the Apple

was something fluttering inside a sconce above the mini fridge behind the cafe stand. The car was quiet save for the low rumble of the engine and the popping of Marjorie's ears. The man with the chocolate bar took his seat, his back towards the line. Marjorie followed the man ahead of her a few steps.

"Hi, can I have an Iced Tea and a blueberry muffin please?" The man held out a visa.

"Sure sir," said the clerk. "So what takes you west?" He took his card for payment.

It was easy for this man to purchase items, like telling someone the time or date.

"Home. Thank you."

He took his refreshments and walked to the back of the carriage.

"A bottle of water please." Marjorie proffered her gift for replenishment.

"This needs a signature."

The clerk returned it to her with a pen making for a ribbon. She wanted to rummage through the words lingering in the air, as to reorganize them into something less affronting.

"Really? Its only a gift card." The clog made her voice sound like a whisper.

"I'm sorry, yes. We require the owners signature on the card being used."

The locomotive, voracious in disorientation, wrenched. Marjorie drove her hipbone into the plum counter. Her sight went cloudy. Broken clouds followed the moon in line. Sodden tissue folded like compact snow. Rhythmically odd horns cawed like some Arctic bird, curdling its way into the firmament. It occurred to Marjorie that madness is a misalignment. Language for things only others can do in gesticulation. What does it take to be here? In the curve of something above you? Swinging in delirium, she signed her given name on the silver strip across her card.

"You are Clement Hackett?"

She clicked back to her flesh at the utterance. She didn't have the safety of familiarity. The words were unmitigated with the lilt that would wake her up for school or preceding a laugh from her mother that could only surface from her first language in conversation. Her dissonant given name being spat into the air landed itself somewhere between the cartilage bobbing in her throat and the lawful ears of Victoria.

How easy it would be to plunge her fingers into her well-trodden duct as to reach her sinew. To peel the skin back and let the twisting nodule drop with a placating thud. It would writhe and harden when it slipped out. The cool grey carpet would be wet with a trail of membrane composed of her phlegm. She stood waft in abject ambiguity.

"Why don't you have your name changed yet sweetheart?"

Victoria was standing between the counter and Marjorie. She couldn't remember when she got there.

"I'm waiting."

"It's an arduous process but fairly simple."

"I'm waiting to be christened."

"You've been already."

"I'm waiting for God."

"I can help you."

"I can't pull my tissue out. I need a new jacket."

"I can help with that too."

"You missed a whole world when you were away. We orbited by a farm of shivering animals. The bridge we rolled through made the room I was in hum. Oncoming trains bolted pressure as they came and went. In your pause a world went by."

JOSS BARTON

Lord, be a femme

Daddie's jacket never fits. The sleeves are too long and the polyester plaid shoulders sag like banal jokes. I'm four-years old and my thighs straddle the body of gender. I want sequins, silk panties, psychedelic poppy prints, six-inch lacquer pumps to click-clack down city sidewalks. I want to be Princess Peach in that 'ol nasty gown and them white satin gloves. I'm constantly sneaking into my mother's closet to wear her maxi-skirts and lingerie. I strip down to Sesame Street underwear to slip on her pink negligee. I envy girlhood growing up. I lust over the lace bows on Easter dresses and I cry when my first tricycle has black handles instead of plastic purple tassels. My femme is tolerated at first for its adorable Kodak moments but it doesn't take too long for my parents to let me know the meaning of the word SISSY. My tiny body twirls in swirls of tenderness and I rummage through momma's makeup bags to find blush kits and tubes of candy apple lipstick. I paint myself as the sissy virus, the transgender prostitute, the bitch hungry for more cum.

—She need mother's milk! She need semen and salt and sick nations on her tongue!! Look at them big brown eyes dripping with pollen. Swear, she's the perfect little piece of queer bait if I ever saw

Lord, be a femme

one. And them cheeks blushing like dogwoods! 'Aint she just the cutest little thing you ever seen?
—Yes, but what about the law?
—What law?
—The hegemonic rules of the state: FEMMES ARE TO POST NO LESS THAN 6 SELFIES TO THE INTERNET A DAY WITH AN ALLOWANCE FOR TWO TO BE TIT OR ASS SHOTS. ALL STILETTO HEELS MUST BE A MINIMUM OF 7 INCHES, DRESSES ARE TO BE SHEER WITH ZIPPERS RUNNING FROM NECK DOWN TO THE TOP OF THE CUNT AND LIPS ARE TO BE GLOSSED WITH EITHER EJACULATE OR MAC LIP GLASS. FINALLY, ABSOLUTELY NO LACE FRONTS ALLOWED.
— Aww, horse shit. No one in this faggot cesspool is free until the femme queens are fucking FREE!! I was a 14-year-old little queer when I began seducing the men in this town posed as a strawberry blonde ingénue with tan skin and cowgirl boots in YAHOO! chat rooms. It was always the same drill:
—A/S/L?
—18/F/MO
—what you doin cutie?
—bored at home, you?
—same, wanna cyber?

These desires are like a train runnin' up and down my back or bowels churning with the weight of dirt black coffee in the morning. My mouth aches with pestilence while wild women dance for disco balls hanging like coked out gods watching from the beams of brown tile ceilings. Where are your children tonight? Have they run down to the brewery gates to smoke pot and break lager bottles against red brick walls? Are they sucking cock behind black shadow walls on winter nights? Are their bellies full with raw meat and sugar cakes? Did you tell them about your youth spent on Missouri porches, sweating during humid summers, drunk on whisky and wet for a man's stare?

— No, that's none of their concern. What would it gain them anyhow?

— Perspective?

— How's this for perspective: His love spread welts across my skin. I try to rub him out like an itch burning inside red eyes, and I dig painted nails deep into the skin to scratch out the trails his tongue left behind. I swallow handfuls of Benadryls waiting for the swelling to recede back down the cracks of my bones to the pink marrow. He ain't never coming back but my body won' believe it.

When daddie asked me if I thought I was a girl I told him 'No'. Tears were in his eyes as he looked on my face. I told him I just wanted to fall in love with another boy. I wanted to take it back, to tell him that maybe I did feel like a girl, that I wished I could renounce the commandments, that maybe I wanted to be something different. I wanted to oppress the lusts of men with psychokinetic hips and pink lips. I wanted a fat ass to roll back in their laps with the power of Delilah. I wanted smooth legs and sore nipples. I wanted to let him know that if I had been given a choice I would have asked to be born in another dimension, where sissies conquered planets and enslaved nations of men hung like Samson. But all I could do was cry while he shook his head and closed his eyes to pray.

CeCe came home today and her release from prison forces me to think about where my liberation leads me. The pig bottom's freedom blooms with the black scent of piss and poppers. Wells of sour chlorine cleanse cum whores as pure as white springs. Even the sub-leather dykes find peace in bandages and bruises but where am I? I'm still here writing about nothing. I'm still an Ozark sissy selling herself short. I'm still poor, brown, and queer. Have I liberated my genitals from the mouths of monsters? If not, then let me bleed out for the viewers at home. My freedom appears at the bottom of

Lord, be a femme

vodka bottles and inside kush blunts. The orange Adderalls tell me I'm young and beautiful in manic mouthfuls as men call to me from online sex ads:

— Hi sexy I have been needing a sexy fem cd I want to have some fun

— Sounds like you've been a naughty girl. When do I get to come over and punish you?

— DAMN, YOU ARE SOOOOOOOOO HOTT!!! I WANT TO FEED YOU MY COCK WHILE YOU SWALLOW MY LOAD OF HOT C UM:

— Damn your body looks good, would like to cum over and play with all those holes.

— Hola sexi, está claro que quiero besar esos labios hermosos.

I'm left to work with these words to find the holy grail of filthy fish status:

— LORD, BE A FEMME! Be anything but a man, be anyone other than who I was told you were. Be a hyena's clit. Be the mother of catamites. Be a bride thirsty for vengeance in a gown marbled in blood. I lie naked on cotton sheets in nude platforms and black nylon thigh-highs. My body is an altar, a dumpster, a crystal ball for binary sins and trans-femme exoticism. The piece of Mexican trade kissing my neck is spotted with black and gray tattoos. He sings 'MAMI' to me in a chorus strung by GRUNT and GROAN as his bare cock pushes deeper down my innards. My asshole becomes a glorious portal through time and space fucked back to Mayan brothels in Guatemalan jungles. The Emperor's warriors visit me while their women net fish and bathe their children in the river. They bring me emerald chokers made of quetzal feathers and young papaya from the trees. One by one they enter my home with cracked teeth and full eggs. Their hands are full with peyote buttons, wild tobacco, devil's trumpets, morning glory seeds, and brown mushrooms dipped in honey. We eat the sacraments and smoke the tobacco to awaken the spirits. They run their fingers through the black hair spiraling down my back. Their breath is heavy with the sour smell of blanché and they growl like black howlers as I massage their scarred bodies with warm oils. I kneel at their feet and pray to Ixtab, goddess of the hanged and guide to Paradise, as I make my mouth a wet nest for their swollen serpents. The heads are the color of ripe pitaya and their flesh burrows down my throat. The spirits gather around my naked body and lift me into the air. The men turn me over onto my stomach and spread my legs to roll their tongues inside me until I'm wet like their women. They stuff me with the tips of thick papayas until the entire fruit begins to disappear into my body. I wail in ecstasy and beg for the serpents to penetrate my soil. The men mount me and grip my neck like jaguars at night. They push in and out, deeper, harder, and faster until the spirits fill their eyes with visions of the world to come: pale demons carrying gold crosses across charred forests, cradles lined with small pox blankets, rabid dogs gnawing on the tits and intestines of two-spirits, CIA operatives chewing coca leaves as they stand at the foot of mass graves. They fill my womb with warm venoms, and I wake to see The Mexican wiping his cock off with my green beach towel.

GILLIAN YBABEZ
Lisa's Story: Zombie Apocalypse

People die everyday but when they don't stay dead it becomes a real problem. Especially when they attack the living. Sometime during the fifth day the internet gave up all pretense and just started calling them zombies.

Several of my neighbors packed their kids and some stuff into their cars and took off. If I had a car, I might have tried to leave as well. The nearest National Guard-established safe zone was a couple hundred miles away. God bless Texas and its open country. Not.

* * *

A couple of days later, the power went out. It was getting worse. Power outages across the country. A safe zone in Kansas had dissolved when someone died inside. Fifty more people died before they were killed for the second time.

The last of my neighbors left the apartment complex. A zombie wandered by the next day and broke into a nearby apartment. One of my neighbors had left their dog behind. The dog got away. I barricaded my front door with sofas and the two big front windows with

Lisa's Story: Zombie Apocalypse

mattresses and bookshelves after that.

I waited for a sign that it was all over. Surely we were pushing them back, right? There was no way mindless zombies could really take over, right? The power might be shut down but that couldn't last for much longer. We couldn't really lose, could we?

* * *

A few days later I realized, this is it. This is how the world ends. I looked out at the quiet apartment complex. I was alone and no one was coming for me.

I counted how many days of food I had left. Seven days. If the stove wasn't electric I could cook rice or pasta – there would be enough for several more days.

I counted my hormone and anti-androgen pills. Enough for a few weeks. I could do without them if I had to but I'd rather not. Would it be hard to break into a pharmacy?

The water was still flowing but how long would that last? I needed to find more water before that happened. I had to go out or die in my apartment. There was a convenience store a few blocks away that would be a good first stop. Beyond that there was a superstore that had to be overflowing with supplies.

But first I had to deal with a problem closer to home.

* * *

When I moved into the apartment, my roommate and I had split the cabinet and refrigerator space. Since the power went out, I had eaten all of my perishable food but hadn't touched hers. Out of obligation to the roommate code I had respected her food rights, even as I piled her mattress against a window. I had believed she would be coming back after finding her father but now I doubted that I would ever hear from her again. I wished I had eaten her food. It was starting to smell.

Sorting through the leftover food I realized none of it was salvageable. I briefly argued with myself over a block of mold-spotted cheese but decided against taking the risk. I repeated the process with the freezer. All the spoiled food went in a trash bag that I tied shut.

I moved the sofas and I armed myself with a baseball bat, left over from that time I tried joining a local amateur team. I looked out the peephole watching for a few minutes before opening the deadbolts. They scraped and squeaked as I twisted the knobs to open them. Had they always been that loud? I made a note to get oil for them. With the trash bag in one hand and the bat in the other I slipped out of the apartment.

Fresh air blew across my face for the first time in over a week. I took a deep breath and looked around. Most of my neighbor's cars were gone. A few cars remained, not that they were any good to me without keys. The neighbor's door was busted in. The door was dented but still on its hinges. The frame, however, was cracked and split around the deadbolt and knob. I turned away, glad that I had remained undetected. I closed the door but didn't lock it behind me, I wouldn't be going far or for very long.

The garbage cans were in the alley between my building and the next. I kept watch on the deserted complex during the walk. Once around back I quickly dropped the bag in a garbage can. Four cans sat in a row, one for each apartment in my building. The one for our–my apartment was almost empty. Two women just don't make a lot of garbage, especially if they recycle like we did. The other three were covered so I couldn't tell how full they were. It would only take a second to peek but I didn't have that much interest. I didn't want to spend more time out here than I needed to.

I turned around and started to walk back to my apartment. As I rounded the corner, I saw a person walk through the entrance to the complex. I recognized the dark blue of the city's police uniform. I should have ducked back and watched. Instead, I walked further into the open. Gut instinct said "don't hide, suspicious people hide from police" and when you're not white suspicious usually means guilty to the police. After hearing numerous horror stories, I had no desire to find out first hand what happens to trans women in jail, so I had always tried to not be suspicious.

He saw me and began walking in my direction. He seemed to be trying to run but his left leg seemed too short and hobbled him. Then I noticed his leg wasn't too short; he was missing his foot. It wasn't a man. It was a zombie. In only a few seconds, it had nearly closed the distance between us. With no more time to think, I gripped the bat in both hands and as he–it got close, I swung at its head.

Its head flew to the side and it stumbled from the impact. I froze for a second, watching it regain its balance until it turned and lunged at me. I raised my bat high and brought the bat down on its head. It cracked and crunched but the zombie didn't fall. It staggered back for a second but renewed its single-minded attack. I swung to knock it off balance one more time before running away.

I ran between the apartment buildings and turned the corner behind my own. Behind me, I heard the shuffle-thump of it following. Looking back I saw it stumbling along faster than a person missing a foot should be able. It will follow me until I can't run anymore, I realized. It won't get out of breath or tired or hungry. I could make it back to the apartment but then what? I have to kill it. I can do this, I told myself. It's hobbled and off balance.

I turned, grabbed the bat in both hands again, and swung as it reached me. It stumbled but this time I didn't give it time to recover and smashed my bat down on its head again. It doubled over from the impact so I hit it across the back sending it to the ground. I circled around to its head and began smashing its skull before it could get up. After a few minutes my bat began to ring out as it hit concrete more often than flesh. The zombie wasn't moving any more, it hadn't been moving for a couple of minutes now that I thought about it.

I snapped out of my killing frenzy. My heart was pounding and I was breathing hard. Looking down at the now mostly headless corpse made me feel ill. I swallowed back my nausea, then I noticed the black gore coating my bat, my arms, splattered on my clothes, and presumably on my face as well. I took a few steps away and wretched.

Taking deep breaths, I forced myself to concentrate on what had just happened. I had smashed in a zombie's head. Should I move the body? Obviously I didn't need to hide it from the police but just leaving it to rot didn't seem like the best idea. Would it rot? These things didn't seem to be really alive. Beside the grayish pallor to the skin it didn't look like it had been rotting and it didn't smell like rotting meat either. It obvious didn't need or have much blood judging by the missing foot.

What did people in movies do with dead zombies? Leave them laying around? If I wasn't behind my apartment building that might have been an option. But I didn't want dead bodies lying all around.

So, I needed to move it, but where? I needed to at least move it away from my apartment building. The complex was four buildings, two buildings on a side facing inward. Parking spaces in front of the building with extra against the back fence. The zombie had chased me between two of the buildings until we reached the back of the buildings where I had stood my ground. The wooden fence around the complex meant I was mostly hidden from prying eyes. Ideally I should remove it from the complex but I had no way to move it other than dragging the body. I decided to haul it to the back corner of the complex near the fence. It would be out of sight and hopefully far enough away that if it did start to rot I wouldn't have to smell it.

I walked back to the body and stood over it. I avoided looking too hard at the ruined mess that was left of the head. Its arms were bare, meaning I had to touch its flesh. Grabbing one of its wrists, I grimaced at the cold flesh. No, not cold, just not warm like a person. It was firm

Lisa's Story: Zombie Apocalypse

and dry, not squishy and wet like the rotting meat I thought the zombies were made of. With a wrist in each hand I began pulling against the body's weight.

It didn't move, at first. I threw my weight back and managed to jerk the body forward a few inches. Again I put my weight into pulling the body and dragged it a few feet before its foot snagged on a crack in the concrete. Slowly, I jerkily dragged it past the apartment buildings to the fence.

My first zombie kill. It had been a lot messier than movies made it out to be. I was covered in stuff that I really didn't want to think too hard about. If I didn't know these zombies weren't infectious, that you had to actually die to become one, I might have been worried instead of just disgusted. I walked back to the scene of the crime and picked up my bat from where I had left it while dragging the body. What if another one of those things had come along? Trying to fight one without a weapon was not something I wanted to think about. I needed to keep my weapons close at all times.

Wait, I thought, it was a cop. I walked back to the body and checked its belt. Empty holster, a couple magazines? clips? of bullets for the missing gun, pepper spray, a small flashlight, and handcuffs. Would pepper spray work on zombies? Probably not but it would work on other humans. I took it and the flashlight.

Once back in the apartment, I locked the door, refortified it, and walked straight to the bathroom.

* * *

Half an hour later I was physically and mentally clean of zombie head gore. I dropped my shirt and pants in a trash bag. Before everything went to hell, I would have tried to salvage them. The pants especially, since before I didn't have many pairs and wasn't exactly rolling in cash. If things went well on my trip, I wouldn't have to worry about clothes.

If they didn't, I still wouldn't need to worry either.

* * *

I redressed for my first trip out into the new world. T-shirt and jeans for ease of movement. A sports bra in case I had to run. My hair was pulled back into a sporty ponytail. I dug a duffel bag out of the closet and adjusted the strap until it was tight against my back. Baseball bat and pepper spray for protection.

I moved the sofas from in front of the door and peered through the peephole. I didn't see anyone. Was I being too cautious? The deadbolts scraped and squeaked as I twisted the knobs to open them. I reminded myself to get oil. From the main entrance to the apartment complex I headed north, staying close to the complex's fence while looking around. At the corner I looked down the cross street. No one in sight. I dashed across the open ground of the first intersection to the relative cover of the nearest house. The smaller residential street I had been following met a larger four lane street bordered by a few small businesses. I stopped by the dry cleaner on the corner and looked around. On the other side of the street was the convenience store. Around it was lots of open ground. Good for me to see zombies, bad for me to have to cross.

The area between me and the store looked clear. Farther away I saw motion in my periphery. At least I thought I had. There was nothing there when I focused on the area. Maybe it had gone behind something. I looked around again, seemed clear. It was now or never. I separated from the dry cleaner's wall and began walking to the convenience store. Across the dry cleaner's parking lot, the four lane street, and across the store's parking lot. I kept a steady pace while looking around, especially behind me, until I reached the front doors.

As I pulled open one of the doors I realized I wasn't the first person to come by. The store was almost stripped clean. I began searching anyway. A package of Snoballs on a rack and a couple cans of beans on the floor. Bags of chips torn open, their contents spilled all over the floor. They crunched under my shoes as I walked between the aisles looking for anything else that had been left behind.

I heard chips crunch behind me. Spinning around, I raised my baseball bat and found myself face to face with a skinny white guy also holding a baseball bat. He flinched and jumped back. I stopped, heart beating fast, teeth gritted, panic flooding my mind.

"Woah, woah I'm not gonna hurt you," he said releasing one hand from the bat and holding it palm out, "I wasn't sure if you were a zombie or not."

My panic faded as I breathed slow and deep. I grabbed a shelf to steady myself as the post panic dizziness set in.

"Hey are you ok?" He looked at me concerned as I tried not to collapse.

"Yeah, just give me a minute," I wheezed.

"Ok, um... I'm Andy," he said.

"Lisa," I replied. Andy's brow furrowed slightly. I cleared my throat, smiled, and said in my most feminine voice, "Hi, I'm Lisa." He smiled mollified by my femme voice.

"What are you doing here?" he said.

"I was looking for water and food." I stood up straighter.

"Why?" he asked, "The water is still running here. Did it stop where you were staying?"

"Not yet but when it does I want to have some water around."

"Good point," he said.

"Looks like you got cleaned out," I said gesturing around the store.

"Yeah when the power went out I tried to close the store but the customers didn't want to leave and started taking stuff. Some of them started fighting, so I locked myself in the back room until they left."

"You were here alone?"

"No one else would work. I was the only one not to bail on my manager. I kind of wish I had now."

"How long have you been here?"

"Since the power went out. A week, maybe a little more."

"Why didn't you just leave?"

"I don't have a car and no one was answering the phone at home. I didn't want to try walking with everything that was going down. What about you, why are you still here?"

"No car either and I couldn't get in touch with anyone." I pointed at the chip covered floor, "Did you do this?"

"Part of it. When they started grabbing stuff, some chip bags got busted open and dropped. I just spread them out. I thought it would help to alert me to someone coming into the store," he grinned at his cleverness.

"You could have just locked the door," I said, "I guess I'm going to have to look somewhere else for water."

"There's a pallet of bottled water in the back," he said. "And I packed everything they didn't take back there too." I looked toward the open door he had come from. "I probably shouldn't have said that. I would share..." he halfheartedly offered.

"No," I said turning back to face him, "You have to protect what you have. I'd do the same."

"Oh yeah," he said, "Hey are you staying some place nearby?"

"Uh... I don't think..." I trailed off not sure how to say, 'I don't trust you.'

"Hey don't worry about it. Sorry I asked."

"No, it's not like that. I don't know you. You don't know me either remember. You have your storeroom with water and who knows what else that you need to protect. You don't know if I'm going to kill you for your water and food."

"I don't think you would-" he protested.

"But I might. You should start thinking like that." I already had, apparently.

Lisa's Story: Zombie Apocalypse

"I should start thinking everyone is out to get me?" he asked.

"Look at this place. They took everything they could and that was before it got really bad. When I spun around, I could have killed you. I almost did out of instinct. I could have taken everything you have." He paled as I talked. I might not be as strong as I used to be but I was still taller and a little bigger than him. "I'm going to go now. Lock the door after me."

"Wait, you can't just leave me here alone," he pleaded.

"I... I can't trust you either. You could leave. Try to find a house nearby to hole up in," I said.

"Is that where you're staying?"

I locked eyes with him, "If you follow me I will kill you."

"What?"

"I don't know you. I can't trust you," I stated. Guess I was over being shy with my emotions.

"Come on this isn't some post apocalyptic wasteland. Everything was normal a couple weeks ago. Why wouldn't you trust me?"

I turned and walked a few steps away from him, putting a shelf unit between us, before turning back, "I'm transgender."

"What does that mean?" he asked confused.

"It means when I was born the doctor looked between my legs and said, 'It's a boy.' and everyone believed him but I'm not."

"You're a guy?" his brow furrowed.

"No, I'm a woman, just – a different kind of woman." I watched him thinking through it. Watching for him for signs of violence.

"You have a dick?" he finally asked.

"Yes," I watched his eyes flick back and forth, his face scrunched up in confusion, "And that is why I can't trust you. Right now you're trying to decide how to treat me now that you know I'm a woman with a penis. You're trying to decide if I've tricked you. You're trying to decide if you should be angry. You are trying to decide if you should attack me."

"I...I..."

"It's ok, I'll see myself out." I walked down the aisle away from him and made my way to the door. I turned back to him and said, "Don't forget to lock the door after me." He said nothing, just watched me leave.

I walked away from the store, past the dead pumps, the package of Snoballs still in my hand. I thought for a second about taking it back as some sort of peace offering for rejecting him. No, I thought, I have the right to be defensive. They've always killed us but now there really was nothing to stop them.

A few hundred feet ahead, a superstore loomed over a mostly deserted parking lot.

JAMIE BERROUT
Three Fragments

1.

It's not until Paz takes her second and third steps inside the dim, cavernous hall of the flea market that she forgets where she's going. Where the hell could abuelita's candles be?

She comes to a complete stop. The floor is soft with a layer of sawdust beneath her high tops. Between the aching blare of the music of the market stalls, which recedes and doubles itself each time she turns her head, and the multitude of lights – the huge fluorescents hanging overhead, the strings of warm christmas lights, the blinking neon signs, and exposed yellow bulbs to highlight each of the different wares – burning in every color she's ever seen and others garish and unknown, and the smell of fried gorditas, heaping plates of tamales radiating steam, mouthwatering popcorn in greasy paper bags (she can practically taste the individual grains of salt) sweetly tart aguas frescas in the clear, icy sweating drums, and racks of fresh pan dulce perhaps still hot to the touch, and the unexpected pleasure, or maybe relief, at suddenly being surrounded by so many people like her, the ones in her family here and in Mexico, speaking in the same accent, same gestures,

Three Fragments

be they lighter or darker than her glowing brown skin, taller or shorter than her small, rounded frame, it's almost overwhelming to merely stand long enough to get her bearings.

But Paz doesn't need to know exactly where she's going, not really, because the memory of the last time she was here, one year ago today with her abuela, seems to draw her forward into the makeshift halls of the market.

It gets easier after a few minutes of walking with her head down, with her phone in her hands and her eyes on the blank screen of the phone – staring at the screen so intently that she could be anywhere else on the planet. It helps keep her calm in the middle of the crowds. As she makes her way toward the rear of the building, the stalls she passes become less popular, more specialized and downright strange.

There. Note the very large man sweating through his tank top and standing ominously at the front of a curtained stall with no sign to indicate what's for sale. Paz does not look into his eyes, it would have felt too much like tempting fate and being trans had already gotten her in enough trouble for this lifetime. At another stall that sells only bootleg Selena tapes and cds she comes closer. Some of them are live recordings from concerts that could only have taken place after her death. While she's still puzzling over the dates she looks up at the five girls behind the counter – Paz thinks they must be sisters because their faces, accentuated by meticulous dark makeup, look nearly identical. The only difference being that the height of each sister is just a couple of inches from that of the next tallest one. All five turn to her with the same tired expression that says, without a word, "What could you possibly want?" But before Paz can smile, they've already turned away.

At another stall, the salesman shouts out his sales pitch, brand new phones he's got, an incredible technological invention of his own making, the only phones in the world proven to not, I repeat, not cause cancer. Paz raises her eyes for a second – they're just old flip phones with alien stickers covering the original brand logos – no, gracias, a

191

wave of her hand. Another stall – sealed pouches of military rations being sold for cheap, but when she veers closer, Paz notices the writing on the packets has worn away – did the guy at the counter even know where this food originated from or was this stuff simply sold from one place to another for less and less cash until it disintegrated?

Because it is their job to observe, the sellers notice Paz walking alone. They see in her a rather unextraordinary girl, not exactly a tourist but certainly not a regular, and make their pitch accordingly. They expect a cordial "No, thank you" or at least a "Gracias" from Paz, but she rarely answers them, aside from nodding or giving a smile that shows her crooked teeth. How rude of her, they must think. To pass by without a word. In fact, Paz is afraid of her voice, or rather, she's afraid of how they will react when they hear her raspy, too-low, untrained, hopeless voice (to use her words) sounding so differently from what is expected of a girl.

Farther on: the lonelier the market seems, the more vacant space separates the stalls, the more dim and irregular the lights become. Finally, it's quiet enough for her to think. Just where are the candles abuelita swore by? Will the old, frighteningly-thin woman who made each of the candles (and was said to be a healer or a bruja) still be there? Will abuelita respond in some way if Paz manages to pray over the candles tonight? Would she go to Paz in a dream or in the form of a forgotten memory? The important thing was to try.

Three Fragments

2.

Nothing changed and all of us lived in fear until the daughter of the Speaker of the House was murdered and rightly eulogized (#hernamewasJosieGarcia) as a trans woman to the great surprise of the conservative party she had been brought up through.

No mere instrument of the party but rather a rising star, Josie had been their future king, their great hope for renewing the party despite its staunchly traditional values. In response to news of her death, the liberal party pledged its support to finding a way to end the rampant killings of trans women of color, as the Speaker's daughter had been only one of dozens slain that year. It was understood that the liberals were sincere in this promise, since they fully expected their own proposals for additional laws on hate crimes and employment discrimination that would, of course, rely on expanded though perhaps ineffective federal oversight, would at last be put to a vote after years of opposition. Never mind if these new policies represented, approached, or even acknowledged the demands made by various organizations of trans people to date, which instead cited such reforms as decriminalization of sex work and immigration and an end to mass incarceration, an end to the institution of the prison even, as fundamental to the rights of trans women. On cable news, the liberals' conciliatory and utterly predictable position was heard twenty four hours a day – this is the plan that suited everyone's interests and had the best chance of becoming law, the public was told, show your support or exit the conversation.

But the most astute political analysts could be heard grumbling at the margins. They said, "This is not what the conservative party is about, they're too focused, they won't go along with it, they'll achieve their legislative goals through the means that suit them best now and over the long term."

Sure enough, even in their hour of despair, amid the motions of the burial procession and the televised moments of silence, the conservative party, communicating through secret meetings and cryptic messages, was adamant in its refusal to concede any victories to the liberal party. Having just lost the White House for a third straight election, in what could only be seen as a stark rejection of their vision (even as they tenuously maintained their grip on Congress) left the conservative party in a constant state of crisis. Without their own president, without the necessary momentum behind them, everything else could be lost through just one concession to their opponents.

Still, political considerations aside, the Speaker of the House mourned his daughter and met with the community organizations Josie had been tentatively joining and giving her support to, as best she could without drawing attention to herself, in her last days. She was remembered fondly, an unexpected champion who cared deeply about the other girls. The Speaker went away devastated by the thought of his Josie rushing about, trying to perform miracles behind his back – there she was donating her collection of books to establish a library at one community center, selling her suits and her car to fund legal services at another, eventually putting her law degree to work by teaching classes to various groups about their legal rights, meeting men that sought her out in the evenings only to push her away before dawn.

The wound remained open for the Speaker, and if anything, it worsened as news came that another young trans woman had been murdered – officially, there was no apparent reason for the violent act, her partner had simply escalated the abuse that he visited upon her regularly, which she could not safely report to any authority or even her family, for she would be blamed for all of it and punished further. The man, her partner, was still out on the streets claiming his innocence to the few who bothered to ask, not because he hadn't murdered the girl (he'd already admitted to that) but because the act itself, the slip of the knife, appeared as inconsequential and natural to him as it did to the police. In the news, the few times the deceased woman was mentioned, statements from her neighbors were quoted to scandalize her memory and erase all traces of her humanity. They did not refer to her as a woman. They said she brought strange men to her apartment. That she must have been a criminal. And so on.

At the moment the Speaker heard of the second trans woman's death, a month late because these murders rarely make the news at all, the girl's friends reported seeing her killer buying groceries as if nothing had happened – he still lived in the same neighborhood as they did, still went by the same stores and bus stops where he first saw the girl he would later kill. A number of blogs carried her friends' appeal for justice, but the police investigation stalled.

The Speaker knew that something needed to be done. He felt this imperative burrow its way into his bones and they ached and ailed him as never before. Even the knot of torn flesh in his shoulder, the result of catching shrapnel in the last moments of his final tour in Iraq – the lucky wound that propelled him to political relevance after an interview in which he commented on the senselessness of that war and of hurting innocents abroad while so many required assistance back home – even this betrayed him as the tissue that had been lovingly reconstructed in a series of surgeries now stiffened and pulsed sharply. But what could he do? Or, more to the point, what could the party agree to?

And so he thought of his wound. And he thought of the weapons of war. And he thought of the gift that the right to bear arms represented to him. He thought of how helpful it would be if transgender women could just protect themselves. If they could wield their own guns. Because if the police and the community can't do it for them let's cut out the middlemen, he thought. But then he remembered the stand-your-ground laws and the system that had condemned Marissa Alexander, who only tried to defend herself with a warning shot, and he guessed the trans women who were being attacked like his daughter, the young black and brown trans women in the DMV he'd met in his tour of the community centers, would also not have the state's benefit of the doubt in the exercise of their rights.

There would have to be something else. The right to bear arms and the right to defend oneself are well and good, he thought, but it's not enough. Like most other laws they are neutral on paper and wildly uneven in application – they simply don't extend the same protection to everyone. There must be a kind of legislative license for these women, some affirmative right to defend themselves, a presumption in their favor that evens out the playing field.

And so the Josie Garcia Amendment was born, a definite victory for the conservatives yet not quite a defeat for the liberals. It was intended to be a narrow sliver of a constitutional amendment, which would hardly affect the rest of the population apart from trans women. All in all, it was a decent and palatable public form of consolation for the Speaker's loss from his colleagues for which he nevertheless had to make enough demands and take up enough obligations that his career was essentially over before the law was signed.

Through the amendment, every trans woman in the country was expressly granted the right to self-defense: that is, express permission to use deadly weapons to defend herself from harm, to issue threats, or to employ otherwise unlawful evasive measures to protect herself. But the heart of the law was an ironclad presumption in favor of trans women, that they could not be prosecuted without federal approval for actions claimed to be made in self-defense, and therefore could not be jailed or arrested for fighting back against their attackers. Instead, trans women were to be held in custody when facing these potential murder or manslaughter charges by the most lax terms possible – here, the law was understood to refer to house arrest in its harshest application, but, more often, to a kind of unsecured (cost-free) bail.

Soon, though, came a startling development in the way courts interpreted the amendment. It was only a few at first but eventually enough lower courts (and their respective circuits of appeal) were

Three Fragments

persuaded to apply the language of the law to the matter of survival crimes, such as illicit sex work and theft and the sale of drugs, so that as long as the defensive, unlawful actions were found to have been taken in the face of some potential harm trans women were protected from arrest and prosecution for these crimes as well.

Lest history forget, it was this development in criminal law, led by trans women of color who fought their cases for years in order to shape the amendment in their favor, that decades later brought about sweeping changes in the ways courts dealt with other marginalized people engaging in similar crimes toward the end of ensuring their health and safety. For even the Supreme Court later accepted the argument that, if trans women should be protected from the horrors of incarceration and if trans women should be understood with empathy as survivors acting in response to the harsh social conditions around them, then why not others beset by different adverse social forces.

Whereas, before, police officers needlessly followed and questioned and attacked trans women, above all sex workers and trans women of color, they now turned and hurried off in the opposite direction at the first possible sign of them. The amendment was so unequivocal in its terms that soon everyone knew a police department could be gutted by lawsuits alleging violations of these new rights.

It goes without saying that not all trans women were protected by the amendment as well as others. That blackness, for example, was sometimes enough to break the presumption of innocence, that race still mattered in deliberating the possible faults of trans women who should have already been understood, under the law, as acting without fault. The amendment was only a kind of beginning and, truly, none of us can predict how the legal system and the conditions of life for trans women will continue to be shaped in years to come by the weight of its presence.

In any case, we can look for guidance to the early days of the amendment's application, when trans women everywhere in the country, individually and in groups, purchased or otherwise acquired guns – reliable Glocks, cozy snubnose Rugers, Berreta nano pistols perfect for a coat pocket or purse, eminently portable polymer Tauruses, pretty pink .380s. They also carried knives and brandished them when threatened and remembered the words of their amendment, "In recognition of the terrible violence felt by trans women, who have been made to live in fear for far too long, who need fear no longer..."

Three Fragments

3.

I couldn't help it. My eyes were drawn to the pink dab of color shimmering inside the lines of the glossy container of lip balm. I looked closer and had the strange sensation that I'd already lived this moment before, that it might almost be nothing but a memory – to have bought the same color, chosen it in spite of my history and whatever others may think of me, and have smoothed the pink, understated and perfect and recalling spring, on my lips.

The lip balm was on sale, and though that helped it wasn't enough that the difference wouldn't have to come out of an essential part of my budget, either a meal or my savings for emergencies, because there simply wasn't money for something like this (discretionary?) that didn't directly contribute to me making it from one day to the next.

It was because of that moment of déjà vu that I bought it, because there was something in that lip color I had tried to forget about myself and needed to remember. When I got back to my dorm and washed my hands, I looked at myself in the mirror for a long time before lightly touching a finger to my lips. The feeling was electric, thrilling, and even more so when I spread the lovely pink on my lips because then I felt the touch run across my body.

After months and months of winter, I felt the layers of damage from all that weather heavy on my body. I'd gotten so used to ignoring myself and everything I thought was possible when I was younger. It surprised me to think there could be more than bare survival. I wondered how long it had been since the last time I touched my lips. How long since I had done something kind for myself?

I wanted to cry. I did cry, slumped on the chilly floor, with wet and careless heaving sobs. I was tired and I let myself be tired. I slept and I woke up feeling new, refreshed, not without hope.

CATHERINE KIM
Fidelity

I.

It is difficult for me to remember what she looked like, to hold her face in my head and keep it still. When I think of her, a part of her is always moving: her freckles slide down from her cheeks to the shadows of her neck; her shoulder-length hair curls up and over her ears; the bits of skin thinnest to the bone draw taut as she opens her mouth to speak. Her eyes quiver underneath their never-open lids. They have a lift to them defined only by the deep stroke of her eyeliner: whether with wire-frames or makeup, or adorned with velvet fingers, they were never naked.

Sometimes she shifts into being someone else: someone I know, someone I don't, someone with or without a name. Her bones crunching down to the height of a schoolgirl, hair twisting into twin braided ponytails, shooting out red string and white plastic flowers. Or a murmur in her chin erupting thin stalks of grey, smooth fields of flesh starving until they've withered, little mountains and sinewy ravines digging deep, as if drilling for veins of oil in her skull. Or— her warm, yellow tones bleaching white, her hair catching embers, her eyelids flicking open to reveal bright green starbursts, knotted in thin, pink veins. Her voice picks up nearly an octave, her skeleton hollowing thin, until she looks and sounds too much like the intake nurse from the night Dad checked me in for a twisted ankle. Cooing sounds rising from her throat like bile while her fingers reach out for my leg. I kick the image from my head but can't think of her again for a while, lest a hint of the girl, the old man, or the nurse remain, in the features I remember of my mother's face.

I used to have pictures of her that I kept close to me: one in a brass frame I'd keep on a small table, next to the fold-out couch that was my bed for the better part of five years. Another, a small one about the size of my palm, in the inside pocket of my favourite jacket: a tiny denim thing that was her May 5th present[1] for me, back when I was still at U.E.S. Reminders I'd keep close to me, near enough for me to turn my head or bury my hand in the folds of my clothes to pick out these—*captured things,* stolen lights burnt still and vivid, polaroids cut up to fit different shapes: mementoes of an outstretched smile, a laugh on mute, the touch of warm hands on numb skin I could think of really feeling with my eyes closed and the cool touch of photo paper between my fingers.

Last night I combed through the boxes Iris had brought up to our new apartment, shuffling through the piles searching for the ones marked up in red sharpie (these were mine; as opposed to hers, which were crossed off in black). They were few in number but scattered, buried in a cardboard forest of her things. I found books with

---

1. A list of May 5th presents I remember my mother gave me, in chronological order: a stuffed doll of an American girl with golden hair and a bright blue dress; a plastic cat with a moving tail and ears and a broken tongue; red velvet gloves; a picture book with horses grazing on the Alberta prairie; a toy truck with flashing lights and wind-up wheels; a silver cross pendant on a thin cord necklace; a kiss on my forehead like an apology and a hymn sung to the rhythm of Dad's mad footfalls just outside the door.

old receipts and torn pieces of note paper bookmarking once-favourite pages, the odd class photo and picture of nothing (a rock, a flowery weed, a blurry yellow thing that might've been a wasp or a bee). A couple photo frames, one empty, the other wearing a close-up of Iris' face (white teeth in perfect rows and parched eyes bruised for lack of sleep). If I had a photo of Mother in those boxes somewhere, I couldn't find it: maybe I'll search again this evening, though I doubt I'll have any luck. The ones I had back then were ones I had kept close, and I think I can remember where every single one of them still were: back in Dad's apartment, halfway across the other side of town.

II.
I'm thinking of this one day in particular, back in Korea, when I visited Pusan, my mother's hometown. She and Dad and I were cramped into a two-door sedan: a battered and burgundy thing smelling of stale cigarettes and fish. Mother had wrapped a couple rolls of kimbap in tinfoil to eat on the way there. I was handing them one by one to Dad from the backseat. He'd drop them in his mouth, eating them whole with lips agape and rice on his chin, before wiping his fingers on his pant-leg; as for me, I pushed out the cucumber bits with my thumb (to my mother's frown) and ate the scattered remainders with my palm.

We were visiting one of her sisters, who still lived in the coastal city, working at a desk in a local police station. This was one of the few times I saw any of Mother's family, as most of them had scattered: her widower father living out of town; a sister who'd call often in Seoul; another sister incommunicado but for birthday letters to my mother and me. I can't remember their names: my mother's sisters were only ever epithets married to nouns. *Professor-Aunt. Writer-aunt.* This one was just an aunt: plain, the default template, stuck from cradle to grave in the place of her birth, just a couple blocks away from the first spark of her sisterhood.

Her home was a narrow thing atop a closed diner-like restaurant, next to a family kitchen that delivered homemade jajangmyeon on a pair of rust-tone, rickety bikes. In my memory, it is only a block from the beach, the alley leading up to the house opening up to water sounds, the tickle of sand in my feet, and a blurred mass of people, cars, crates, stacked together and shifting: children atop metal boxes, cranes without bodies, roads with bouquets of stop-signs and traffic lights bursting from the weathered pavement. It is the impression, or the dream, of that beach that I hold—and I can't say I know how to measure the distance between a real place and a dream.

I remember that her smile was thin and worn often; that she looked like my mother with heavier eyes, and wore muted colours as if she were always stuck in a state of mourning: there were bright, even colourful things in her home, but they were odd, even violent protrusions, never quite settling in their place atop a cupboard, a shelf, or a bedside table.

Auntie seemed to slip in almost too easily to the dynamic between my parents, like a warm, pulsing sliver penetrating skin. I thought that I'd never met this woman before (though later, she would show me a photo album with shots of her holding my naked infant self above a grey wash basin, which felt like the sliver had buried itself home). When Mother misplaced something she had meant to bring in her many bags, and Dad's temper started to simmer, Auntie silently took me out next door to the noodle kitchen where a kindly woman with a mess of shockingly white curls gave me a small dish of white noodles in spicy red paste: we shared it on the bottom step of her house, the door closed at the top and the old kitchen woman watching by, as she told me stories about my mother's childhood that I didn't believe.

Later, in the evening, after my mother had shooed her away from

Fidelity

the dishes, she took me into her room and sat me on the single mattress she used for a bed. In front of me, taking up most of the wall, was an ornate cabinet with intricate patterns on the doors, the crisp colour of the wood faded into something duller, but still huge to my girl's height. Inside were clothes, packed tightly against each other, many still in their cleaner's wrap. She showed me her old school uniform, the irregular buttons my mother had sewn in to replace those whose threads had frayed and let them fall. She also showed me a traditional Korean dress, a hanbok: pocketless, with smooth colours, in white and a bright, mint green.[2] Small piles of clothes ended up on the bed and on my lap, my fingers running through their fabric, her hands guiding mine to different textures, wispy ribbons, smooth silk, and plush, soft cotton.

From that day I am left with little cuts, nicks on my knees and elbows from playing on the dirt road, and slow-burned images that I have visited time again, unwittingly in dreams, directionless in thoughts such as these. I remember thin walls with glassless picture frames; the heated floors; the cupboard television with many stations; the metal rice bowls with lids I nearly burnt my hands on, earning me my aunt's concern and the privilege of my Dad's fingers, stretching out mine before his eyes to see how red they were. The mosquito netting my aunt cast over the blankets in the study, before I turned in for the night. Falling asleep to the tune of whispers, clattering cups, insects and dogs, and creaking wood. There are enough of these little cuts to make the absence of that place feel like a more permanent wound, a real place outside my little world that I have

---

2.. I've seen my mother in these clothes in a wedding picture that I think was left at my grandfather's place. There were two photos that I remember in particular: one of her and Dad kneeling with stone faces in these beautiful, garish clothes; another, across from that, with her in a white western wedding gown, complete with small train; Dad was in a suit and dated tie; I think, in that one, they were smiling.

touched and lost: enough for me to envision myself as an impossibly small girl looking up at columns of closet doors standing giant in front of me, piles upon piles of clothes bulging out and spilling like clumps of blood by my outstretched feet. School clothes, silk garb, a worn winter coat with a rich fur collar; a cadet's uniform; a military vest; an old wedding dress with a long, jagged tear on its front.

III.

We had stopped for gas shortly before arriving at Auntie's place; Dad had just left to buy a pack of cigarettes while the attendant was filling the tank. Mother turned around in her seat to face me, speaking in a hushed voice: she called me by my full name, and rapped the back of my hand when I continued to play with my doll. She said: *Be careful around your aunt*. I think careful is the best word for what I remember, though she didn't mean careful *of* her, but *for* her: *she's the only sister without a husband*. I must have nodded, because I remember her reaching out and cupping the side of my head, rubbing my cheek with her thumb, which was something she used to do often when I failed to reply aloud.

IV.

It was once important for me to remember these people, these scatterings of names and memories: they were one of the few links I had to my mother. However tenuously, I thought of going back to Korea someday, visiting the places of my mother's childhood, her coming-of-age next to the sea, a beach of sand, of rocks, of barges and industrial ships tearing through murky waters. At the very least, I thought I might call—say, on a birthday, either hers or grandfather's or one of my aunts'. Some day in which it might be a touch more reasonable to call after having kept more than a decade's silence, a day in which the date would be all the justification I would need.

Of course, I haven't called, or made any plans, looked up any flights. It was a childhood dream of mine, much like how I wanted to don a blue uniform and a badge without thinking of the weight of a gun in a holster on my waist; or wanted to wear a long white coat, garb myself in Mother's pride, without any mention of green gloves splattered with rust and a beating heart quivering with its last hints of life in my palms.

I'm thinking of this one day in particular. I'm thinking of kimbap rolls and noodles and melon-flavoured ice cream pops and the soft bite of twilight air. I'm thinking of the blur of the countryside dotted with the odd farm: the ones I remember look nothing like they do in the Canadian prairies. They are thick blue tarp and clear plastic sheets and black dirt and paper homes. If there were any giant rolls of hay dotting impossibly rolling hills, as if they were grazing on the luminescence of the grass, I don't remember seeing them there: maybe this is a selective thing, differences between my two nations more sweet to my memory than droll repetition. Regardless: her house is a journey from a journey to me now, a place in a place that is not here. It takes effort for me to think about it clearly: she is a dim thing, sleeping beneath a low ceiling, bathed in nothing but quilted blankets and candlelight.

V.

Iris dreams of peach cotton dresses and denim jackets and a five-dollar cupcake smuggled in her girlhood purse to the drab office of some faceless clerk (to her, where fantasies hit the ground, she takes off running). There are no bells in this dream; no stone churches atop verdant hills, no virginal bridal gown to trip her feet on the way to stained glass and an ordination. It is furtive and secret and all the more precious for it, like whispers on collarbones against the shelves of a filing cabinet (lights off and phones on silent), or hands clasped beneath the table surrounded by frigid backs and cooling dishes. After her dream, she wears her ring on different fingers by the day, and loops mine in a cord around my neck and pulls me to her. Someday, she says, her sister will come back from burning change in Portugal and her father will dig his way out of his papers and his liquor and if they are not proud, they will at least be resigned, and to her—to whom romance is cherry suckers and cheap shoes and reasonable weather—that is enough.

VI.

The wax is running out. I can hear the pattering footsteps of the upstairs neighbour's children. These walls have not yet been baptized by the smoke from an endless chain of cigarettes: the absence of that smell is still something new to me. The ringing of that day grows faint, muted, like a bell on a ship sailing away; though my mother's words, in their native tongue, still echo in my head.

manuel arturo abreu
Collecting

It's not exactly dark out when they gather in front of Fine Fare at the corner of Gun Hill and Perry. The sky is steely blue and blushing orange. They are armed with black shopping carts and white garbage bags. From some blocks west comes a whoop with echoes, then a piercing whistle. There's the blanket of hum that all cities emanate. The smallest girl is squinting across the street: Perfect Pose HAIR DESIGN, Rosario CIGARS, IMAGEN UNISEX, Tropical SUPERMARKET. Her mother yanks her by the shoulders away from the curb's edge. The younger son is still gone.

    They have a routine at this point. The father takes the older girl and the younger boy; the mother takes the younger girl and the older boy. The father walks northwest; the mother walks southeast. They scour the entirety of Norwood and meet at the Williamsbridge Oval afterward. They use train stations as markers of distance or progress. The father's team walks to the Woodlawn station, the last stop on the 4, collecting along the way. They walk south toward the Mosholu station, excavating everything west of Reservoir Oval W. The mother's team walks first to the B and D station at 205th, then toward the 2 and 5 Gun Hill Rd. station near White Plains Rd., and finally back toward

Collecting

the park. The two groups double-check, take every turn possible, look into every alley, walk into every open basement area, rip open every garbage bag, dig into every trashcan. They double-check their double-checks. They always wear white latex gloves. They work until an hour before the children have school, that they might have a moment to quickly wash the Bronx off of them, get ready, and get there.

Nickels "add up." It's zero-sum. Other collectors soon learned to loathe this family, would try to awaken earlier than them, assemble teams of people they trust to run a similar operation, but five in the morning's amazingly early and five other trustworthy people are incredibly hard to come by if you don't have a family. They would be left to scavenge whatever the family had missed, or, more plausibly, was generous enough to leave behind, because anyone with any respect doesn't pick every fruit from the tree. Industrious latecomers would hunt at the outer limits of the neighborhood, or even way down east past White Plains Rd, or west when W Gun Hill Rd becomes Van Cortland Park South. Jerome Ave curiously separates Van Cortlandt Park from Woodlawn Cemetery, some folks walk along it as if they were going to Woodlawn Heights, checking for discarded bottles at the roadside.

Amateur collectors who aren't worth their weight in bottles talk endless shit about the family without ever having met them. The family moves about too much to hear any of it. Their brilliance lies in that they don't only collect cans at dawn. After the father has returned from work and the children return from school to finish their homework, the family goes out for a shorter, more fine-grained two-hour run. It constantly accumulates, and if it could be done someone would collect it all day. They return home to eat dinner and relax, whatever that means in a one-bedroom apartment for six. From the father's industriousness and minimal know-how of carpentry came a split living room and a split bedroom such that the inner half of the living room became a small bedroom for the parents; the inner room of the bedroom was for the two girls, the outer for the boys, each with an iron bunk bed and a murky window. The view is a brick wall decorated with pigeon shit. As well, the father and the boys go out before their nightly showers for a quick run, an hour at most, swift and exact. Their routine is just about perfect because at the hours of their runs, no other potential collectors are on the street: in the early morning, they're in bed; in the afternoon they're preparing and eating dinner, and probably watching television; at night they can't even think about going out, as they're preparing themselves and possibly others for bed. Collecting is something other people do, sometimes, but the family has made it one of their keystones. It may not be their reason for having come here, to the Bronx, but whatever that reason might be, collecting would do for now. The father has been saying that for five years.

Dozens are milling about the reverse vending machines, flies are buzzing about the garbage bags, children are hurtling about everything. Everyone's waiting for the family to finish disposing of their afternoon run, of course they've accrued so much that it's taking them some time. People are looking at each other, at the family, at rogue clouds. For a second the sun is behind an advertisement. A lean, cut boy in a tank top and big jorts does pull-ups on scaffolding in front of a condo across the street. A man and a woman, both with their arms crossed, look east down Gun Hill, at Kennedy's Fried Chicken & Sandwiches, at the carpets hung up to sell.

"It's ten cents there," he says.

"Where that at?" she says.

"Michigan, I want to say."

"I thought it was California, is what I heard."

"Well, Cali ten cents for bigger bottles, Michigan they just got to be non-refill."

"Let's go to Michigan then."

"Man, this ain't Seinfeld, come on now."

"What's that?"

Collecting

"Just a white person show."
"Seen."
"They try it and it costs more than they can collect."
"Damn. Man, damn they be taking mad long every day."
"They collect the most. It's the most. It's like, ask them, be like, what you did today? You know what the answer gon be."

    The family has aged into their routine. They are a family of backs of hands: check the dirt under their fingernails. Speaking in absolute terms, American poverty for them is lighter, though not easier to manage, and lonely. The father knew: at home, you are a man, with people. Here, you are a shadow, trying to avoid being stepped on, fumigated. The mother knew: cheap chain food joints made it easy and greasy to eat one's feelings. The parents had decided to give up what they knew so that their children might know something else. Or they just wanted to see what it was like. Maybe something else could be paved through a different kind of struggle, if roads are anything more than walking feet. The older son, who immigrated with his parents at eighteen, is essentially resigned to his expired work visa, lack of English, and mason work, saying "the papers will come soon." He works, in fact, alongside his father. Depending on how much work is available, they sometimes work up to fourteen hours a day; sometimes less than five. The mother cleans homes, asks for strictly cash payment, has no papers, no alien registration number, nothing. The two girls have entered Catholic school, they dare not put their fingers in keyholes. When they aren't too busy with homework they help their mother cook. The younger son— he walks towards the apartment building in jorts that dribble down him like yolk and pristine black Jordan Sixes. A woman is fixing her son's pants after having helped him urinate behind the many-mouthed blue cloth of the scaffolding. Before the younger son's mind is an instant he recalls vividly, from when he was much younger. He is collecting with his father one summer morning in the whispering light before the sun becomes a hot angry eye. He screams at a dead rat on its belly and his father hits him on the shoulder.

"Be quiet, boy. Don't see your sister screaming do you."

"But it's a dead rat!"

"Exactly. It's a dead rat. Now quiet yourself."

He remembers something else: in sixth grade he had been suspended for being involved in an amateur explosive-related incident in a school toilet. His father:

"Smart enough to make a bomb but not smart enough to use those smarts productively, eh?"

"It was just a trick Pa."

"Who got tricked?"

The older son, in the Bricklayers Union, had not yet come home for the night. He is young and spry and, for now, an asset to his employers. The entire week the younger son had been missing, but it's not as if the family was going to stop operating because of his lack. His father noticed absently and flicked his eyes away. His mother's fingertips became raw pink from biting her nails. The first night she had deformed her sleep cycle, staying up until the pre-dawn collection, believing he would come home at some point, but after crashing into her bed and sleeping the entire next day away, she knew she couldn't alter anything in her life for the sake of vigil. It wasn't church. He was gone, and he would come, and if he didn't, he was gone.

He does come. A turqoise-and-orange squirt gun is on the black-and-white tile of his building's lobby. He looks at the elevator. There were brazen pennies in the bars covering the window, when he was younger. He looks away. His hand gliding along the railing, he climbs the two sets of stairs, jiggles the keys in the door. He smells chicharrones from outside it. As he enters he sees from the tiny foyer his father sitting in the armchair reading a Pentecostal interpretation of the Bermuda Triangle. Bobby Medina, the Pentecostal singer, is playing unintrusively in the stereo. The younger son walks into the living room and his father stands up, smacks him in the forehead. The boy's

Collecting

left hand flails to the wall for balance.

"Explain," the father said.

"Yeah, I know. Look, I know. Did the school call?"

"Yes, of course they called, mariconcito. Said it's been more than a week."

"Okay, listen to me." A grimace of a pause from his father. His mother at the threshold of the living room, the kitchen steaming.

"No, what you been doing? Where you been going?"

"Just listen." He breathes in, his hands covering his mouth.

"It's really simple. Like, ingenious. I'm no longer going to school. I don't need it for what I been thinking. And I been thinking it's not gonna be helpful even if I do do it, I ain't about to get hired by a corporation, and I ain't trying to work in McDonald's. So here's the idea: I'ma collect full-time from now on. Think about it: I'll meet up with the rest of the family for the daily collections, but then I can forage on my own throughout the rest of the day as it accumulates, eating along the way, probably bring some food from home around in a backpack, course I'd come home and sleep sometimes, when I absolutely have to and if it's an hour where there's not much to collect, and the money would be for all of us to find a way to use, of course there are ways to use it since nickels add up, and I could even collaborate with other collectors throughout the day, we could start building a wider and wider network, really I think the plan is great because the money basically collects itself, not like garbage is something America lacks, it just needs a living walking vessel to carry the containers and deposit them, and maybe there could be more large-scale stuff with other neighborhoods— well —"

His father's eyes are two orbs of horror.

JEFFREY GILL

Two Stories

1. Untitled

I've just gotten off the phone with my Grandmother, "Mom, mom," I call her. We had a two hour long conversation, ranging from her commentary on horrendous cafeteria food to truly validating statements in response to my overwhelming emotions. My Grandmom raised me, thus we've experienced a lot together. She is possibly the only person who can wholeheartedly understand me; she's crucial to my identity. On the phone she stammered, "From the beginning of your existence... Jeffrey, your life has not been normal." Toward a lot of my sentiments, I feel almost guilty. How *dare* I feel this way, as if it is unjustified, baseless, without any provoking factors. But my Grandmom's words were reassuring, that the way I feel is perfectly reasonable, if anything, it's expected. With her words comes immeasurable courage, a protective hand cupping my trembling wrist, a message unknowingly preparing me to tell my story. She asked me if being transgender was the root of my inner turmoil; I explained to her that I'm still deciphering through each piece of sadness, trying to see where everything stems from. With such twisted fate, I unfortunately have a handful of ailments which muddy together and, in my head, become one. I don't know where pain begins and ends, it makes it difficult finding anything. Tomorrow I cannot simply wake up cisgender and revel in the contrasts to the day before – I do not know what it's like to not be trans. Can I truly understand the impact it has on my wellbeing if it is the only truth I've had?

Within me is an intense curiosity. *I want to know.* This has sparked an awareness of my environment, myself included. From a very early age, I have always thought of myself as "aware." What this means exactly, I'm not too sure. Translating my emotions and feelings into tangible sentences has always been a daunting task, however, this awareness is an elusive quality that I'm proud of nonetheless. Inevitable for me, through the process of becoming more aware, I am creating myself. I began by visualizing myself from outside my body – an onlooker watching from a distance, I then realized that who I saw was not the person that I was perceived to be. Albeit quite conceptual, the "person" I saw was not necessarily seen, more specifically it was an emotional response to an energy I felt. I didn't see someone whose blue eyes replaced my brown ones, or whose pale pink skin replaced my own brown skin, no. More so, watching myself, I did not recognize the aura I would otherwise associate with the Jeffrey I imagined myself to be. Needless to say, this marked the beginning of my awareness of self.

On a night in my 12th summer, I experienced what I now know to be a schizophrenic episode. Lying in bed, anticipating falling asleep, the typical late-night thoughts spiraled into chaos. My mind became so loud, I became so scared. A voice not of my own crept into my mind. Who it belonged to, I'm still unsure. Its tone was undoubtedly cool, the way someone sounds when they know something that you don't. Taunting me, it yelled: "You're a girl! You're a girl! You're a girl!" I spoke back denying the accusations, though the voice only grew louder. "Yes you are. You're a girl!" Back and forth we yelled at each other, and for how long this went on in actuality, I can't say, but in the moment it felt like forever. Begging for sleep, and for this to end,

I yelled back louder than the voice coming from inside my head, "No I'm not!" As if waking from a dream, instantaneously the paralyzing voice vanished. I lay in my bed hauntingly still and painfully silent, as to try and not disturb a single thing, an attempt to dissolve into my blankets, to hide in plain sight. Only my heartbeat reminded me I was alive. I fell asleep and woke up the next day paying this experience no mind. For so long I kept it at the back of a hidden drawer inside my memories, the kind you disguise by filling it with socks and underwear – I suppressed it. Actively I wanted to forget it, and until now I practically had.

When I entered high school was the very first day a boy caught my eye. It was the lunch period, and I had to figure out the daunting task of finding my lunch table. Watching the stampedes of hungry students around me, my gaze stumbled upon a very attractive boy. Tall, with short, dark brown hair. When my eyes fell upon him, he was already looking at me. I immediately assumed that he was gay and, him being the only gay person that I could see in "real life," I felt an innate connection. I later discovered his name was Jason.

Every day, we passed each other in the halls after my first period gym class; his eyes unapologetically watched me the entire time. I never looked towards him, even though I wished to. On my birthday in October, blowing out my candles I wished for him to approach me. When I finished my slice of cake, I walked back into my room, to see a message from Jason on Facebook. I thought that I was hallucinating, how this could possibly be? I do not know. Certainly this was a reminder to believe in the Universe. It was really him. We chatted the entire night. Since we shared the same lunch period, we would meet every day in a small corridor just before the gym locker-room. There we would hug one another, and talk in private. I remember the first time we met there, I was so nervous, I didn't think it was physically possible for my palms to be so damp of sweat, but when we returned back to the cafeteria and to our respective lunch tables, my eyes were brighter and boy was I giddy!

Our relationship grew closer and more intimate. He was older than me and around him I felt safe, important, and beautiful. I would spend weekend nights at his house, what I remember most from these nights is the feeling of his heaviness on top of me. Kissing, bathing, and lounging was what constituted our listless time spent together. I only let Jason see my body in the dark; I hid my penis from him as much as possible. He never touched me there. I never felt comfortable with him paying attention to that, it would physically repulse me if he accidentally brushed over it while we were nestled together in bed. I would flinch. I enjoyed his touch, but not there.

I am not disgusted with my body, I desire no alterations to it (at this moment), but even then at that young age of fourteen, I knew that, superficially, the penis defined someone as male, and I didn't wish to be sexually acknowledged as a male at the most literal form. I have never had any other intimate encounters since Jason, but I think this sentiment will continue to follow through each partner I grow close with. Often times I imagine myself with a female, and while I feel open to the possibility, it is especially triggering. As if she will make me innately more masculine, more heterosexual, more cissexual male. Everything I wish not to feel, or be regarded as. This repels me from pursuing a relationship with a girl. Perhaps this same force that does not allow me to traverse sexuality freely lends me to imaging myself with a more virile, dominating masculine man. The idea of me being with someone so much more masculine-appearing than I am makes me more feminine in comparison. This is a damaging thought process and ignorant too, something I wish to abandon. As I accept myself unconditionally, I believe this barrier will diminish and I will be able to feel comfortable in a relationship with someone anywhere on the gender spectrum. Although, saying that, I find it to be too rosy: However content and proud I become of myself as a trans individual, still I suffer at the hands of an unwelcoming society.

Two Stories

I am instilled with fear; this is something I am certain stems from my trans experience. I am incredibly conscious of everything around me, a hypersensitivity to every environment I enter: a particular glance, the minute change in a pitch of a voice, sudden quick movements and loud noises...all of it I'm constantly aware of. Is my fear purely cognitive, an illusion unprovoked?

I would not completely disagree, it is undeniable I do bring a certain amount of pain upon myself. A form of unwanted, incurred masochism. But growing up, I read many nonfiction horror stories in the news, experiencing mild ones myself. They perpetually reminded me that the streets are not safe for those like us, that this world was not made for us. My awareness and constant guard are here for protective circumstances, allowing me to never feel too comfortable because that comfort could be dangerous. Resembling that of the nature of a doe who can never graze freely in her fields, both ears are constantly detecting the small vibrations through the air; she can never enjoy her meal; a predator is always lurking. It is incredibly tasking on my heart to always feel uncomfortable in public, specifically around men, whose stares are often times unapologetically abrasive and harassing. My Grandmom tells me *the world isn't made for sissies*, but to what purpose? How much must we endure, do we continue until we succumb to death?

From my earliest childhood memories, I remember other young children asking me whether I was a boy or a girl. Whether this was sincere curiosity or intended as a crude remark, I always interpreted this as an offense.

2. A Short Work of Fiction On the Nature of Daylight

He woke me up, said that he could hear the sun rising. In his voice I searched for comfort, and lazily I found a convincing likeness of it. With the white curtains giving into the soporific light filtering through, I rested my cheek on his drunken cheek and together we munched on the strawberry sky.

Listening to the sounds of the surf grow louder, with him I lingered in bed longer than usual. I can recall the faint sound of his breathing, barely audible, just enough to let me know that he was there with me. I could imagine us floating in a bubble across the sky, impenetrable to time and space. During that brief moment of daybreak, he allowed me to forget the war and cruelty inside myself.

We had met the night before. I was spending the summer in the Mediterranean, on the island of Mallorca. When I wished to descend the mountain and head towards the sea, in the early morning I would have to ride on small mules and travel the hard, tedious road. It would take about an hour of slow travel, through the red earth paths, the rocks, the treacherous boulders, through the silver olive trees, down to the fishing villages, made of huts built against the mountain flanks. Some nights I would wish to stay down on the beach, at times sleeping atop of the sand with the crabs, washed-up shells and other debris. On this particular night, I had trouble falling asleep and decided to partake in a walk along the edge of the sea.

I leaped from rock to rock, the soft lapping of the waves at my feet. I ventured far from my habitual beach, and came across a small, hidden cove where the moon hung low, placed almost artificially in its pool of stars. I stood there, mesmerized by its splendor, and could sense the sound of someone near. I could see a head bobbing in the water and occasionally an arm. I watched them, and found solace in our shared sleeplessness.

Instinctively, they called out to me with a lightness, "Come in and swim. It's beautiful." It was said in Spanish.

Speaking to the moon, I asked, "Who are you?"

"I'm Benjamin," called the voice from the sea, "come and swim with me."

Tempted, I looked all around, with only the stars filling every inch of night, we were certainly alone. And with the view from those rocks as magnificent, the calm water reflecting the white light ... I decided to join him. I took off my linen shirt, now well worn and scented with the smells of day, slid into the water, and with long easy strokes, I made my way towards him.

He disappeared underneath the water and soon I felt him grip his arms around my legs. In the water we teased one another and, wrestling like flippant dolphins, he dived under and between my legs. We came up for air, laughing nonchalantly, and I swam towards and then away from him. My loose pants, worn to keep me cool during the day, began to rise and bunch around my waist. Hampering my movements, I took them off, and was left naked.

I floated and he swam beneath my arched back. Suddenly he embraced me from behind, covering my whole body with his, easily I became aware that he was naked too. The water was warm, it felt like we were sharing a bath, and so salty that it bore us, helped us swim without effort.

"You're beautiful," came from his deep voice, arms still around me.

I thought of floating away, but the warmth of the water held me like the soft slip of his wet skin. My body was languid, I remember closing my eyes. Now between my legs were his hands. And while his caress was as warming and lulling as the water, I tried to swim away. But he followed, grabbing and mounting me from behind, kissing the small of my neck at every chance he could get. Struggling away from him only made me more aware of his body against me and his hands upon me, and if I had continued with such constant motion, he wouldn't have been able to take me, but the touch of him aroused me and I grew weak.

I swam toward shore, he followed, and we fell on the sand. The sea washed over us, its waves coming ashore to die, its foam lubricating and cleansing our sleepless bodies. That morning, when I woke in his bed and dawn broke early, the sky glistened. Everything was drenched in sunlight and with him by my side, I saw him clearly now, distinctly. Brown and amber-hued, his face had a softness to it, as if it were blurred at the edges. Benjamin had green eyes, eyes greener than the sea, and his lips were irresistibly pink; ripe and sweet like hanging fruit. With the horizon on fire, those wet lips of his kissed me again and again, and somewhere deep inside me, womb-like, I felt a warmth stirring. I wished for him to consume me whole; I'd wished this wish before.

It was immediate, we decided then that we would meet on the same shore each night long after sundown.

How many more times we met and fell on that sand, I'm unsure; time has always been a concept I've had a hard time grasping. But sometime before I felt the familiar inconsolable urge to go, he told me that a poem he'd written, which I admired, he'd written for me. No one had ever made me the muse before.

Something inside me shifted. You see me. I am finally seen. It takes so little, really. How well do we see someone who we know only for a brief while? How well do we ever see anyone at all? I know too much and I know nothing at all.

I had always been expecting someone — every open of a door, walking down the streets, the reason to go out to that party, each time I entered a cafe, a theatre. There was this calling for me to be in the midst of another, I wanted to be seen. My cravings were vague, poetic. I was expecting the spectacular and, in spite of this, no one lived up to the expectations of my desire. I traveled in search of love.

Two Stories

Paris and its metros, the passersby on the cobblestone streets along cafe terraces, the shared silence of crossing quays. New Orleans and its streetcars, the blistering heat, us all moving in slow motion, the cacophony of jazz and footsteps. Montreal, New York, Lagos. And Deià, the small idyllic village that lurks my memory today of days from almost fifteen years ago.

Now here I am, back on the same beach, feeling the same moonlight on my skin, the warm water carrying with it the tastes of that summer. As if the mere power of thought can bring out the physical manifestation of desires within my mind, I think of him profusely; it makes me feel ill, predatory. I am someone who hunts and loves without consent, a masochist who leaves before they are left all while wishing to stay. I think of Benjamin; like honey, he sticks and I lick him from the concaves of my memories. And memories disappear fast, they are forgotten. That's the way things are.

LIBBY WHITE

Back Home: Three Short Stories

1. Don't Go

"Your skin is such a beautiful brown," I crooned, tracing my fingers across his bare chest. I loved watching him breathe. The subtle rise and fall of his breast. His nipples, dancing up and down like two horses on a carousel. He breathed such a nervous breath, so short, my Marcus. Gazing out of our hotel suite at the New York skyline, he held me in close, just breathing, blinking softly, and sighing. We lay there for a while, naked, pressed against each other on a bed wrapped in satin sheets. I played with his nipples. Marcus just gazed at the skyline.
    "Baby," I said as I kissed his damp chest. He didn't answer. I sighed and curled into him. His arms wrapped around me, one hand cupping my chin as I watched him stare out of the window. Away from me. "Marcus."
    He grunted.
    He always got like this after sex. I bit his chest.
    "Ow!" he yelped as he pushed my head off of him. He watched me, wide eyed. His eyes screamed betrayal. It made me giggle.
    "Are you hungry?"

"I don't have money for room service," he said, suddenly too pissed from being shaken from his moody musing.

"I'm not asking for money baby-"

"And anyway, I have to go." He rose from our bed, already slipping on his work slacks and buckling his belt. I crawled to him and tugged on the back of his pants until he looked at me.

"Why?" I purred.

"Why?" He was in another world, snatching himself away from me and throwing on his shirt. "Are you really asking me that?" he said, almost to himself. His stance, his confused look, his pouty lips. It amazed me how well he feigned incredulity.

"Baby-"

"Don't do that." He was already buttoning his shirt. Damn, he dressed fast!

"What?"

He stopped in between buttons. "Just don't, Kamil."

Suddenly, I was a little too naked for the brotha so intent on leaving. I got up and grabbed my boxers off the floor. "Oh, so I'm Kamil now."

He struggled with his socks, as always. His muscles were too big, too defined from his years in college football. Elbow perched on a corner table, he was squatting and trying to use both hands to pull a sock over his left foot. I sucked my teeth and stalked over to him. But when I reached out to him, he swatted my hand away.

"I got this," he said, without even looking at me. So I watched him. I watched him struggle, stumble, almost fall. I watched him, foot tapping, arms crossed, sneering at the nigga. He didn't fall. He got his socks on, straightened up and remembering that he left his shoes by the door, pointed them out to himself and went to slip them on. I watched him the whole way.

"Yeah you go right ahead brotha," I taunted as he passed.

"Will I be seeing you in service tomorrow?" he asked, slipping his shoes on as comfortably as socks. Well, as comfortably as socks for other people.

"Maybe." My gaze fell to the carpeting. Persian? Maybe, Syrian? " I don't know."

His tie was on an expensive dresser made out of the kind of dark wood one uses to show off. He grabbed it.

"Come on, Kamil." His fingers worked so quickly over that double Windsor. "I thought we agreed on this."

"I'm just," I couldn't stop my arms from falling to my sides. "I don't feel well. I'm thinking I might go by the doctors tomorrow." I looked up at him. Him back at me. He straightened his tie and swallowed, his gaze even.

"You can go after."

"No, I can't." He knew I was uncomfortable. I shifted too much. He passed me again back to the other side of the bed. His face grimaced when he found nothing there and looked around the room.

"You left your jacket in the taxi."

He nodded and headed back for the door. I stepped out of his way.

"Don't you want to know if it's an appointment?" I asked, eyes closed.

I heard him stop. No turn. Just a dead stop between the door and me. I could hear brass jostle. Was his hand on the doorknob?

"No, Kamil, I don't." The knob turned as the door creaked open. I opened my eyes and slipped between Marcus and the door, slamming it shut with my body.

"It's one appointment, Marcus." His eyes were closed now, his head turned away from me. His jaw set. I cupped it with my hands and brushed his cheeks with my thumbs. "It's very important to me. This is my health."

"I don't want to talk about this right now." A child.

"Marcus-"

"I don't want to talk about it, Kamil!" he grabbed my hands and

229

pulled them off, grabbing the doorknob again. I grabbed his shirt with both hands and pulled him into me.

We were still. For a moment. I breathed into his shirt. He swallowed hard, breathing over me. So nervous, my Marcus.

"Baby," I sighed. "Please, just listen." He yielded to me then, his hand falling from the doorknob, holding me at my hips as I spoke into his chest. "I know you want to leave. I know you do. You have... stuff you have to do. I get that, but..." Every muscle in him drew itself tight. "Please. Please don't leave here angry." I raised my head off of his chest and stared into his eyes. Too soon for him, perhaps. I caught him off guard, as his beautiful hazel eyes pooled with tears. I placed my hands on his cheeks. He trembled at my touch. "Because if you do, baby, I'm scared you won't come back."

He swallowed again, hard. His eyes fell from mine. "I don't want you to die, Kamil."

"Pfft, Marcus, I'm not gonna –"

"Baby." His voice shook too much. His form trembled too much. There was a fear to his voice. I tried, but I couldn't laugh it away. "Please," he begged. "I need you to listen to me."

"I'm listenin." I stroked his face as he locked his gaze with mine. A tunnel, it felt like. A tunnel into his soul, a soul too deep not to fall into. How many others lay captive at the bottom of those eyes?

"Baby," he said. "I'm scared."

I laughed a fake and hollow laugh. "Scared of what?"

"Scared of you. Of losing you."

At least one. At least one captive lay at the bottom of his fears.

"You mean so much to me," he said. "Too much, I-" He thought for a moment, then shook his head. "Just come to church." He pulled my hands from his face and lingered a bit before releasing them completely. "Pray with me and the congregation." He smiled, warm and kind. "God will save you," he said.

"Marcus," I tried to smile as earnestly as him. "You know God ain't want nothing to do with me."

"Kamil-"

"That's enough, baby." My hand was back on his chest. His smile had faded. I grabbed his shirt in my hand and pulled him into a kiss. It amazes me how soft he becomes. How supple. "Now you've gotta go," I wrapped my hands around his tie, straightening and tightening it to his neck. His chin rose quickly in response. "You've got a kid, remember? And a wife?" His body immediately firmed itself, shoulders squaring, jaw setting. "And what do they need from daddy right now?"

"A smile." He smiled.

"A smile." I didn't. Not a real one anyway. I patted his chest.

"What's your sermon going to be on tomorrow?" I asked.

"Forgiveness."

"Apt," I chuckled. He didn't. He was staring again. At the door. Through the door. His lips were trembling. His shoulders were sagging.

"Kamil, what am I going to do when you're-"

I grabbed the back of his head and pulled him into the crook of my neck. A sob, pulled too tightly from his gut, wracked his body. He shook against me, hard. His chest beat against mine his labored breathing, his desperate gasps.

"Be with God, baby." I closed my eyes, trying to believe. "And hopefully, when all is said and done, he'll bring me back to you."

I tried, really hard to believe as I held him. I kept my eyes closed as tightly as I could. *Behind these lids*, I thought. *Surely behind these lids I can find it. Hope. Faith.* But I couldn't.

I just couldn't.

2. Mike Lee

Mike Lee smokes Cools cigarettes. Mike Lee smokes Cools cigarettes and blows smoke rings. Sometimes he links them. Sometimes they make him smile. Mike Lee is only 25, but all the old people on our block shake their heads at Mike and use him as the bad example their grandkids should never look up to. The kids listen. They don't speak to Mike.

Mike Lee is 25 years old. A smoker. An African American. A drug dealer.

Kids know to stay away from Mike. Mike tends to stay away from kids. Actually, Mike tends to stay away from everybody. An ironic trait for a drug dealer. I often wonder how he gets his customers. He often tells me not to worry about it. So, I tend not to worry about Mike Lee.

Mike Lee didn't start smoking Cools at twelve. His father didn't buy him his first pack. Mike waited patiently, like any law abiding citizen, until he turned eighteen. And then, on December 22nd, 2010, Mike took his line walking ass down the street to the corner bodega on Paine Ave and bought himself a 12 dollar pack of Cools. On the curb outside the bodega, Mike smoked that pack dry. Seven years later, I sat with Mike and shared a pack with him.

"I don't know how you do it man", he said, taking a deep drag out of his cigarette and blowing out the side of his mouth. Away from me.

I hadn't finished lighting mine yet. "What?" I paused to ask.

"Write for all those people man." He blew, again to the side, and chuckled, punching my shoulder. Friendly. "You know they don't give a damn about you. About any of us."

Two small kids in windbreakers walked up the street toward us. They were on their way home. Mike watched them, watched their little book bags bobbing up and down behind them. Watched them make jokes and push each other. He watched them notice him, his chin rising as they drew near. Mike nodded at them and smiled, but they scuttled away from us. They would rather cross the street than cross by Mike Lee.

"I don't know," I said. Mike didn't smile. He just stared ahead at those kids, watching them watch him. "I just do it I guess." The smoke burned my throat when I took my first drag. I coughed, buckling over, spitting onto the sidewalk. There was nothing to show. Just saliva. There was nothing wrong with my lungs. I didn't do this kind of thing. Mike patted my back anyway. "I don't have a choice," was all I could say.

When the kids passed from sight, Mike Lee turned to me and stared me in my eyes. It was then that I noticed how gray his were. Pained. Tired and far past my bullshit. He shook his head and looked away from me, taking another drag. "We all got choices." His exhale was long. Smoke billowed from his mouth and lingered around his face. He blew it all away.

"You chose dealin'," I asserted.

Mike nodded, ashing his cigarette. Mine was burning out, but I hadn't been taking any drags. I'm not a singer, but I felt like I had to save my voice for some reason. Mike watched me stare at my Cool, took it from my fingers and put it out in the curb.

"You chose them," he said. And suddenly, Mike Lee didn't look so tired after all.

I straightened myself out and glared at Mike. "No I didn't."

"Yes you did." Another drag, another exhale, more smoke. He watched me glare at him. There was no anger in his eyes when he spoke his next words. "You got no love in you man." He leaned back and continued to smoke the last bit of his Cool. A car was coming up the street. A Mercedes. "You think you do, but you lost it." He flicked his cigarette into the street as the Mercedes drove over it. Night was already descending over us. The streets were quiet. The bodega lights illuminated Mike from behind, casting a glow around his frame. "You ain't gonna find it with them."

"And you found it dealing?"

Mike chuckled and shook his head again. As he watched me watch him, I wondered if he saw a glow around my frame too.

"I never lost it," he told me.

We sat in silence for a long time. And when it hit nine o'clock, we stood and watched the bodega close, its owner, an older Dominican man, pulling metal slats down over its windows and front door.

"Buenas noches, Hector," Mike said. And the man smiled and quickly nodded.

I don't think he noticed me as he passed.

"Goodnight!" I shouted. But he didn't look at me. So I watched him. I watched him walk up the block to his car, a beat up station wagon. He opened the car door and looked at us one last time. He shouted in Spanish. Mike shouted something back. The man laughed, got into his car and drove off.

I turned to look at Mike, a wide grin cast across his face. He pulled out another Cool, lit it, dapped me and took off his own way too. I shuffled off. I didn't have the heart to watch Mike Lee anymore.

3. Under the Lights

I'm holding both sides of a small television that barely works, in a Trenton apartment that barely insulates me from the cold, staring at the screen and begging for some proof that any part of this interview was worth it. Me, so underdressed in my jeans and t-shirt. Diana McAvery, in a full light blue pant suit that caught the light of every camera that captured her.

"And with the recent deaths, um, murders and suicides of trans women, do you find yourself more afraid for your safety?" she asks, head cocked to the side, her face awash with piercing compassion.

"Um..."

It was a mistake to do this show. I know this now as I watch myself squirm in a high backed sofa, flooded in so many lights, and boxed in a medium close up shot that makes everything look way too big for me. I'm like a mouse, too afraid to look directly anywhere but down and at anything but my hands. I look so confused, which is ridiculous because what is so confusing about her question?

Yes, Diana. Yes. I feel so unsafe when trans women are murdered and forced to kill themselves. But *more* unsafe? Like what, like this is new to me? Or at all? Like if I didn't see all of these graphs and news stories and statistics projected around the stage, none of the threats, assaults, or comments I've experienced would have been enough? Or mattered as much?

No, Diana. No. I don't feel more unsafe in a world that hates me because I'm black, hates me because I'm trans, hates me because I'm a woman, and hates me because I'm not a man just because you just started finally seeing it too.

But do you? Do you feel *more* unsafe? Does it frighten you to see the fragility of so many lives shattered by the negligence of an apathetic country? Does it concern you to be reminded of the systematic ease with which this machine can chew every rich morsel of your worth

235

and spit out your body like plaque when it no longer has any need for you?

I watch my face as I join my recorded self in feeling these questions churn around inside me. There I am, the tragic trans girl, ever uncomfortable in a lavish studio set. Unsure of what to do with the kindness of a concerned white woman. Out of place in clothes I was asked to wear.

It's a casual sort of interview, her publicist told me. *No need to dress up.*

And so there they had me, in my favorite pair of jeans, in my favorite System of a Down shirt that took me an hour to iron, in New Balance sneakers I rarely wore. There they had me, sitting next to a glowing Diana, makeup aging me too much, lights catching me too little. Everything around me making me appear so small.

It was a mistake to do this show.

"Jules," she calls me, my name rolling off of her tongue so coolly. In one word I was reduced – a child in a supermarket being reprimanded by a parent who doesn't want to embarrass herself. In one word I am petulant, uncooperative, unreasonable.

"Yes," I say, and a mournful groan can be heard off screen running through the audience. The video cuts from my face to a close up on a woman silently crying into a tissue as her sisters hold her. I later learned that they weren't planted, but when I sat there, watching the crowd, I couldn't help but feel so plastic. "Seeing so many trans girls-"

"Um, heh, trans *women*, Jules," Diane corrects, chuckling with a friendly grin. "Let's not reduce them." The audience chuckles with her then, a camera panning over their forgiving smiles.

"Sorry, Diana," I smile, folding my hands together and making eye contact. I clear my throat when my eyes find the floor again. "Seeing so many trans," I pause and look to the audience as a widescreen from overhead displays us all together. How like friends we are. "*Women*, dead or dying in a world that doesn't seem to care –"

Back Home

    I cut off the tv and go to bed. I know what comes next. Diana and I play softball with some transphobic apologetics and then have the calmest and most flaccid conversation about hate, murder, and rape I've ever heard in my life. Then we talk about race. It's riveting.

LULU TRUJILLO
Space Hunters

"GOD THIS SUCKS!" Penny complained, brandishing her beer in a drunken rage. In one quick gulp she finished her drink and called for another. She slammed her head onto the bar and let out a groan, her black hair spread across its surface, her brown eyes red with tears and tanned skin covered in dirt and grime. It had been more than a week since she and the rest of the crew of The Arbiter had been grounded for repairs and in that time there was no news about a prospect for a new job. All the crew could do was sit and wait for things to turn around. Penny groaned and slammed her fist, the barkeep giving her a warning look. "I just wanna be back in the sky already…hate being grounded."

"Shouldn't be too much longer Penny Baby. Repairs are almost done." Penny looked up to find the captain of The Arbiter, Gretchen, giving her subordinate a sympathetic look. Penny blushed and tried to make herself presentable to her boss, but Gren (as she liked to be called by her friends) let out a loud laugh from her large belly. Gretchen had been the captain of The Arbiter since its first flight twenty or so years back. A motherly figure, she was twice the age of Penny and older than most of her crew, but she still could hold her own with any one of them. Her dark skin shone in the bar lights, and she always seemed to tower over the people she surrounded herself with. It helped she was taller than most folks, and wider to boot, but it only helped to give her this gentle feeling that her crew liked to brag about. Even with her size she never looked down upon others or tried to intimidate, as easy as it could be. Yet if someone needed to be taught a lesson or a fight needed to be fought, you could always see Captain Gren standing tall and ready to end things. "Don't worry hun. Shouldn't be too much longer till my contact gets here."

"Contact, Captain?" Penny asked. Her captain simply pointed behind them to a rat-like gentleman that had just walked into the bar. His clothes were covered in grime and filth, his skinny body seemed like it shouldn't be able to support his weight, and his graying hair and long beard did not help his appearance one bit. While Penny recoiled a bit, Gren called the pauper over.

"Ey' Gren...been a while since I see ya. What, like, ten years o' sothin?" asked the man, taking the seat next to the captain.

"More like five, Pugs. Last I saw you was on Nubenegra, if I remember right. What takes you to this side of the universe?" The man gave a toothy grin and smiled.

"Wa' else? Treasure to be 'ad here. There rumors, ye see, bout an old derelict ship ou' there. Centuries in the void maybe. Ancient. Alien stuff...could be worth a fortune. I got no ship but...let say I take 5 percent o' the cut an' I'll talk for ye..." Gren looked back at her pilot and smiled.

"I think that's a pretty fair deal Pugs. Why don't you and I work on some of the details? Penny, mind checking up on the twins for me?" Penny nodded and shot out of her seat, thankful she no longer had to deal with "Pugs" anymore.

The space port was crowded with the wanderers and vagabonds of the known universe, looking for their next big stake. Aliens from all over flocked to this oasis, hoping to hear even the whisper of a rumor, knowing that it could lead to the next big score. Yet though most were there for the hopes of treasure to be found, there were very few incidents of murder or sabotage. What made this more surprising were the many types of people that gathered, who normally would be at one another's throats at all other times. Humanoid bird creatures were seen discussing engine troubles with carnivorous lizard men, and humans were talking to an ancient species of insect-like creatures that only a century before were at war. Scavengers, no matter the race, always stuck to their code to get the most of their adventures. Trouble would bring the unwanted attention of whatever government was in charge of the sector, and the bigger chance of them finding what the hunters themselves sought. Yet above all else there was an unspoken code among them, that if broken would only bring ruin to your ship and crew. The first to claim it are the ones to own it. In truth, it was less like hunting and much more like a race to see who could get to the goal first, and Penny had no intention of losing to anyone.

After wandering around the many ships docked, dreaming of one day hooking up some of the parts she saw from them onto her own ride, she came across their own ship, The Arbiter. Penny looked up lovingly at the ship she had piloted for the past few years and called home. It was a very old ship, (though the Captain liked to call it a classic) that had seen its share of travel. The hull was covered in dents and scars, showing the many close calls the ship had come with pirates, meteors, and the occasional ramming into other hunter ships. It was painted an emerald shade with black highlights, and on the prow there seemed to be the remnants of flames that were hastily painted on. The captain would always get embarrassed and would mumble, "Dad always thought the flames made it go faster" when the subject was brought up. It may not be the youngest ship in the universe, but Penny felt like it could outclass any newer ship they came across. A small eruption from one of the engines made her rethink her assessment, as she rode the tram into the ship and ran to the cause of the explosion.

"I TOLD YA NOT TO PRESS THAT SWITCH! MORON!" Penny heard a shrill voice yell.

"IT AIN'T MY FAULT YA DIDN'T HAVE THE GEARS IN PLACE! IDIOT!" She heard an equally annoying voice respond. Penny walked in to see two young kids, each indistinguishable from the other, tumbling around the engine room punching and biting one another.

"Hey! What the hell is going on?!" Penny yelled. The two on the floor looked up.

"AH! PENNY! THEY STARTED IT!!!" the twins yelled in unison. The two stood up and faced the older woman, still side eyeing one another with contempt.

"Dakota, Harley, what in the hell is going on here?" Penny asked, unhidden frustration poisoning her words.

"Well Harley was too busy looking at their shitty toy magazine to pay attention when I told 'em to press the button!" yelled Dakota.

"Well I would have been more attentive if Dakota wasn't busy playing around with their shitty game and remembered to place the gears in fast enough!" Harley roared back. The two tried to go at it again, but Penny grabbed them both by their collars and hoisted them off the ground, at arm's length from one another. The twins, Dakota and Harley, were identical in almost every way. Both very short and very lanky, their bright blond hair and their piercing green eyes made them seem very much like a pair of porcelain dolls. If only they were as quiet as dolls, thought Penny. Gren had found the two geniuses on some backwater planet, trying to make a nuclear engine in a dumping yard. Since then, like Penny, the two joined the small crew and usually spent time either tinkering with the engines, or trying to find something else to tinker with.

"Look you two," Penny said at length, "Personally I don't give a shit about this. I want this engine fixed now! The Captain is getting a job for us now and if this ship isn't ready to fly by the time she's here, I'll..."

"What will you do, Penny dear?" asked Gren, who for someone so large was still able to sneak up easily on the pilot.

"Cap...CAPTAIN! I mean...uh...I mean..." Penny bumbled, letting the twins drop and putting her hands together nervously. Gren laughed and patted the young woman's shoulder.

"Don't worry hun, I got us the job. Babies! I want you to fix this room up ASAP! It's time we go hunting!" The twins high fived and went to work. Gren looked again at the young pilot, still too embarrassed to do more than fidget with her hands. "Penny Baby. I need you to get ready to fly. Knowing Pugs we won't be the only ones on the hunt. You ready to race?" Penny's face lit up, her heart beating fast knowing her Captain needed her.

"You can count on me, Captain!"

***

"Maaannnn this is boring..." Dakota complained, sitting at the navigator's station in the cockpit. In the center sat Penny, leaning forward in her motorcycle-like seat, hands on the throttles.

"If you're bored you can join your sibling in the engine room," Gren suggested. Harley's face filled the screen in front of the crew, a scowl painted on their face.

"You can keep 'em! I don't need no help from a loser like you anyway!" They stuck out their tongue and hung up, causing Dakota to spring from their seat. A cold look from Penny made them reconsider. Penny looked starboard and saw another ship pulling up to the side.

"Captain..." Penny started, but Gren held her hand up.

"Didn't think ol' Pugs would keep his mouth shut..." She mumbled to no one. A screen popped up in the front of the cockpit, and an old human man looked down at the small crew.

"Greetings," the man said in a voice used to talking down to others. "My name is Captain Jefferson. I am in control of the St. Ann, fastest vessel this side of the galaxy. I would recommend you turn away from this, Captain Gren. I don't think your…'ship' would be able to handle the pressure." Penny's face flushed red, and she could hear Dakota grinding their teeth in rage. Gren simply smiled and looked at the older man with cold eyes.

"Thank you for the concern Captain, but I think my ship and crew are more than capable of keeping up with your lovely ship." The old man harrumphed and shook his head.

"That is where you're wrong, Gren. My ship is top of the line; the finest of power cores, five engines running at a solid two hundred percent more power than your own and to add the cherry on top, the largest crew a captain can ask for. What, pray tell, can your junk pile and pitifully tiny crew do to stand up to my own?" Gren simply shrugged and reached for the control panel.

"It's very simple sir. What my ship lacks for in power and my crew in size, we have one huge advantage. Simply put…we're better than you." With that Gren hung up on the man before he could reply back, leaning back in her seat with a smug smile. "Show them we mean business." The captain ordered. Penny revved the engine, fire bursting from the back. The other ship did the same, the two waiting for the signal. A beeping noise came from the console in front of Dakota.

"Captain! Probe's back! We have a hit!" Gren smiled a wicked grin.

"FULL SPEED AHEAD! I WANT THESE FOOLS TO SEE OUR TAIL END THE ENTIRE WAY THERE!" Without further prompting, Penny pushed the throttle forward and the ship sprang to life. It sprang ahead of its rival, who lurched to life and followed suit, pushing its engines to the max. The two ships were neck and neck for the first half of the race, The Arbiter pulling ahead ever so slowly past its rival. In response they rammed the side of the ship, causing The Arbiter to shake and groan. Penny couldn't tell if the scraps of metal that came off were from the other ship or theirs, but a fury roared in her heart as she saw her baby being hit. Penny called for Harley to let it all out in the engines, and pushed the throttle farther still, till it couldn't anymore.

The crew was thrown back into their seats. Stars far off flew by instantly, and the asteroids seemed to be closing in faster and faster as they entered the field. Even at this speed Penny was able to easily avoid the incoming space rocks, dancing around gracefully past the incoming debris.

"The beacon is getting louder!" yelled Dakota. "Should be dead ahead!"

"Keep her steady Penny! We have only one shot before the bastards catch up with us!" Gren pulled out her console and with a stick, took control of the only gun on the ship. Penny lined the ship up for its shot, and with expert precision Gren fired their marker onto the target. A moment passed until the familiar ping echoed through the ship.

"We got it!" Dakota yelled, their fist shooting up with excitement. Gren took a deep breath and leaned back in her seat. Penny slowed the ship to a crawl, seeing their rivals turn tail and run to look for their next hunt. Harley ran to the cockpit to see what they had caught, and the crew gasped. A ship as ancient as the planet Earth itself, and as large as a small city. The young crew members stared up in wonder, still excited by the hunt. Gren chuckled and approached her pilot. She leaned down and kissed Penny's cheek, her face instantly as bright and hot as a sun.

"Now..." Gren said, grabbing hold of the twins in each arm, "Time to see what we caught. Penny I need you on standby! Start loading up the arms and get us close to her hull!" She plopped the twins down and patted each one tenderly on the head. "Harley I need you suited up and ready to board in five. Dakota, I need you to stay on comms and make sure we don't get lost out there. Let's see what we can plunder, people!" Gren clasped her hands and the crew got right to work.

Penny slowly moved the ship close to the ancient derelict and extended the "arm" right through the hull. In the dead of space, Penny knew she couldn't hear the crunching and shattering of the rusty metal as the drill dug further into the ship, but a shiver went up her spine none the less with the thought of it alone. Dakota, for once, was quiet at her seat, preoccupied with making sure all communication systems and scanners were functioning normally. They had done this many times, yet Penny knew Dakota was very protective of their sibling no matter the situation. A crackling could be heard above their heads, and a voice boomed out from the PA system.

"Penny Baby, can you come down to the air lock for a moment? I need some help here." With that the voice cut short and the deck was silent again. Penny jumped from her seat and rushed to the captain's side. As she walked, she couldn't help but fret about what could be wrong. Maybe the airlock wasn't working, or perhaps there was a leak in the oxygen tanks. The more she thought on it, the more Penny went from a fast walk, to a jog, to reaching full sprint in less than a minute.

"CAPTAIN! Is everything alright?!" Penny dashed into the room, her head bowed down with exhaustion and her lungs pining for air. A tiny laugh caught her attention, and Penny saw Gren's face contorted in pain, trying her best not to laugh. Penny couldn't help but blush hard as the dam broke, and Gren let out a full belly laugh. Penny's face grew as red as a tomato, and in a huff she turned her head away.

The laughing soon stopped to be replaced with the dull noise of the engines of the ship. The redness in Penny's face had subsided a little, yet she was still upset at her boss...didn't she care at all about how much Penny was worried? Her answer came a moment later, when Gren's chest pressed gingerly against her back. "I'm sorry honey. I didn't realize how worried you must have been. Next time I'll be sure to be more specific to what I need." Penny leaned back into Gren's soft body and let out a small contented sigh. The light press of lips against her neck made her giggle, the red of embarrassment on her face drained and was replaced with the red glow of love.

"Well... I suppose I can let it slide this one time," Penny said, turning to face her captain. She noted that Gren's space suit was not quite fitting. It clung tight to her stomach rolls and was still very loose in the upper body area. Penny raised an eyebrow and Gren could only give a sad shrug in response.

"Doesn't fit the way it used to. Only a year or so ago I'd be able to do this part myself." Gren turned and motioned to the latches on the back of the suit. A few towards the top hung around and jiggled with Gren's movements. Penny sighed and worked to close the clamps, having a bit of difficulty closing them up.

"Gren I think it might be a good idea to cut back on the late night snacks." Penny grunted and she forced the first of the clasps closed. Gren laughed and shrugged her shoulders.

"I thought you liked me this big, Penny Baby. Didn't think you would like me to slim down." She gave a wicked grin as Penny blushed furiously, quickly finishing her work.

"It...it's not like I want you to get slim!" Penny yelled out, and felt embarrassed for reacting so quickly. She took a deep breath and held Gren closer to her. "I just want you to be safe Gren... I want you to come back safe to us." Gren lifted Penny's face to hers and looked lovingly at her pilot. She pulled her in tighter and kissed her gently, laughing slightly as she felt Penny lean forward on her toes to get an even deeper kiss.

As much as Gren would have loved to stay like this, there was work to be done.

"GREN! ARE YOU ALMOST DONE?!" Harley's voice called from the air lock. Gren winced, pulled away from Penny, and shrugged as the younger woman whined. "Sorry hun, duty calls. Let's make up for this when I get back, alright?" Gren gave Penny an affectionate squeeze before heading to the air lock. Penny waved goodbye as the doors closed and frowned slightly. She knew Gren would be fine. Harley, as annoying as she was, was able to take care of their self and was very protective of everyone when they went scavenging. Sighing, Penny slapped her cheeks and pumped herself up. She had a job do to do and wanted to make sure Dakota hadn't made a mess of the bridge by now. With renewed vigor, Penny dashed back to the main deck, the thoughts of treasures and adventure soon dispersing the worries and fears from only moments before.

SAKI
Untitled

Lonely, lovely blooming maple treacle with coconut cream. Counter of local hipster diner-style establishment. Said pudding sits on the counter for an expensive three ninety nine the gelatinization actually a product of agar agar lecithin and similar ingredients, probable designated all-natural superfood antioxidants.

    Walking past the window the realization hits that the lack of nourishment of the past few months have really taken their toll the taxation high and even I am willing to go all in with pocket coins for this experience. My two friends stay back for summertime chats about my strange sudden need for diner product but that's ok as they are kind enough for this exercise. Their names largely irrelevant but their hair and clothing a kind of pastiche of an aquamarine black and yellow their personalities one a mix of quiet sadness a sort of roundness to her words and actions the other one essentially a groundhog in human form.

    Walk in.

    Pause. Too many questions whose answers were questions whose mothers were never born. Booleans regarded as the end-all function, booleans regarded. Emotional booleans, but I come in with my ternary logic and everyone stares. Oh, how everyone stares.

Untitled

The local people an insular sort though loud objections would be had of a politely shocked variety if this were brought to their attention. Shine a sunny spotlight on the boundaries of the world. Situation gets more and more tense especially as notice begins of outside associates and their decidedly non post-graduate bearing.

God comes in like "I'm an infinite dimensional being immanent in all space," and everyone laughs at what a loser he's being. The subject of our shared plight The Divinity and Me sadly leads to no solution for our current mess, for him today there will be no driving of money changers from the temple. When I was born there was nothing wrong with me a ticking little clock (maybe) but everyone has that. Opulent luminous persimmons go around the tables, sliced thin with plenty of pluots dried in the morning sun to follow.

Alto and soprano appear all pianissimo from behind the cash register. They throw me out and I can't really blame them. Crystal harmonies and all while your hertz go in the negatives.

Decisions, decisions what does one do lots of questions here. But the clear answer is skating a large amount over all the tables crushing the tables and grabbing the coconut cream dish for myself and my now rapidly manifesting "buddies". Home cooking some dishes is really acceptable here but really acceptable is not really what is desirable.

Piano piano piano piano.

Quick consultation follows this quick deterioration of the plan to exchange cash for goods and services. Purity of purpose is often desired but it is basically impossible. I convey some details of the plan but being minimal here don't want to involve them too much in my nonsense though they are angered ready to start some noise. To make your tincture beetles.

Just get ready and do it. All people are ready to do it. I am ready to do it. Do it. Jump in. We're all waiting.

This maneuver: An interesting problem in contour integration with several poles to avoid and an unusual topological structure given the table table counter jumping required. Failed attempts at essential singularity creation (by others, in or near my body). Amazing the world of tones that breaking glass causes, experimental symphony with careful calibration would be graded well on an art school final. Solution sums to the desired outcome, got it.

A variety of emotional responses are experienced widely varying based on the individual experiencing them for example: outrage, glee, puzzlement. These selfsame individuals are now the most prominent emitters of noise and shouts in the immediate vicinity. I am a low emissions vehicle.

Trailing, a wave to be outrun lest we become surfers. Groundhog friend is the best runner by far. Now the weapon of starting to think what is a good name for a chihuahua pet it younger and younger the baby animals will get their due.

Flirty flowery and positively anechoic the hiding place is safe. Impromptu marathon leaves us all breathless and collapsed and we are done for the day.

The sad friend laughs, an uncharacteristic twinkle in the voice like little sparks flying. What the fuck was that you nearly got us killed. Oh yeah but look at this sweet mango cherry sauce thing I scored. Quiet laughter and applause all around for the sweet mango cherry sauce thing. Maple treacle also gets in on the show, though unfortunate coconut cream was spilled.

Okay, listen here, whoever and wherever you are. No, seriously.

We are all crushed. We are crushed and there you go. The earth is colorful and loud and wet. But when we look out at the moon we see that all your tentacles reaching out there are a little bland, why is it looking this way? It looms, it flattens, it disappears. Whenever you realize that other beings could be lurking outside you you find it hard imagining. We are connected. We are connected and we sing.

Kiss me on the lips sapphire and maybe this will all disappear.

ABOUT THE AUTHORS

BOOK ONE

Michelle Evans is a Black trans woman currently living on the East coast. A freelance writer and aspiring fantasy novelist, she only occasionally exists and is not quite convinced the whole causality thing is actually real

Vita E. is a trans poet and percussionist from Cleveland, OH. Vita's passion as a Black Trans artist, activist, and educator, has led to the start of many milestones; from being a finalist in the Capturing Fire Poetry slam in DC, to being a member of the Chicago BTGNC Collective, and the Black Lives Matter Chicago Chapter. Her response track to Janelle Monae, "Hell Y'all Ain't Talmbout," was cited in The Source's "10 Songs Soundtracking the #BlackLivesMatter Movement." They are currently a proud member and drummer of the Chicago Latinx Punk band, Cabrona. Vita's YouTube channel and brand, TWOC Poetry, seeks to create positive representation and advocacy for the experiences of marginalized people, which is informed by their experiences as a NeuroDivergent, Queer, Black Trans Femme Artist.

Carla Aparicio is a Panamanian trans woman writer and aspiring psychologist who is, at long last, happy to be here. Her dream is to help other LGBTQ+ folks dealing with mental illness.

Dane Figueroa Edidi, dubbed "Lady Dane, The Ancient Jazz Priestess of Mother Africa," is a Black Trans, Cuban, Nigerian, Indigenous, American author, singer, dancer, actress, writer, playwright and curator. I am the first Trans woman of color in D.C. to publish a work of fiction as well as the first Trans woman to be nominated for a Helen Hayes Award.

Olive Machado is a Cuban, Nicaraguan, Chahta, and Tsalagi trans lesbian writer of fantasy and science fiction.

DM Rice is a non-binary author from Dallas, TX who received hir B.A. at the University of Houston. Zie is a staunch proponent of the singular gender-neutral pronoun, despite its naysayers, and hopes that its instillation as a linguistic fixture will improve public perception of trans people everywhere.

Kylie Ariel Bemis is a queer Native American trans woman trying to decolonize academia in the no-woman's-land of computer science and informatics. She is a two-spirit, a hacker femme on the autism spectrum, and an enrolled member of the Zuni tribe.

Venus Selenite is a 2016 Bettering American Poetry nominee, a 2017 Pink Door Fellow, and an editor at the Trans Women Writers Collective. A Louisiana native based in Washington, DC, she is the author of trigger and The Fire Been Here. As a writer, interdisciplinary artist, and sex worker, Selenite tours and creates work throughout the U.S. and previously acted in Dane Edidi's Absalom (2015) and For Black Trans Girls Who Gotta Cuss A Motherfucker Out When Snatching An Edge Ain't Enough (2017).

About the Authors

A multi-disciplinary artist and writer, **Serena Bhandar** writes with inkless instruments on paper that cannot burn. Her poetry, essays, short stories and art have been featured in publications throughout North America, and often ponder the intersections between minds, bodies, genders, and space. She currently lives and works on unceded Lekwungen and Esquimalt territories in Victoria, Canada.

Emmy Morgan is the author of *The Ice Princess* (2016), the first in a trilogy of books about a black gay man who comes out as transgender later in life.

BOOK TWO

Ellyn Peña is a multi-disciplinary creatrix from Texas, residing in Chicago. They are an avid knitter, crocheter, and fiber artist. Her goal is to create platforms and communities of trans women valuing each others work and lives, creating freely and lovingly.

Jasmine Kabale Moore. Writer. Bookworm. Shares a birthday with Toni Morrison. Follow her at comegently.tumblr.com and instagram.com/comegently

Joss Barton is a writer, photographer, journalist, and artist documenting queer and trans* life and love in St. Louis. She was a 2013 Fiction Fellow at the Lambda Literary Foundation's Emerging LGBT Writers Retreat and was an exhibition artist for Nine Network's 2015 Public Media Commons Artist Showcase. She is also an alumni of the Regional Arts Commission's Community Arts Training Institute. Her work has been published by Ethica Press, Vice Magazine, HIV Here & Now, and Vetch Poetry: A Transgender Poetry Journal. She blogs at www.newamuricangospels.tumblr.com.

Gillian Ybabez is a thirty-something year old trans Latina and a writer of fiction. She wants to write more stories of all genres about trans women existing. This is her first published story. More of her stories and her blog can be found at www.Gillian-Ybabez.com. Look for an expanded version of Lisa's Story: Zombie Apocalypse and other stories in the future.

Jamie Berrout is a writer and translator from South Texas. She lives in Southern California and blogs at desdeotromar.tumblr.com. She is an editor at the Trans Women Writers Collective.

Catherine Kim writes fiction. She was born in Seoul, South Korea, and emigrated to Canada at a young age. Follow her blog at maudeling.tumblr.com.

manuel arturo abreu (b. 1991, Santo Domingo) is a poet and artist from the Bronx. They currently live and work in Portland, OR. Find them at twigtech.tumblr and @Deezius.

Jeffrey Gill is a young college student from Baltimore, Maryland. Their interests range from quantum physics to making the perfect cup of tea. They enjoy reading poetry and having critical conversations about social issues. Jeffrey's primary goal is to give and receive love.

Libby White is a Black Cherokee transwoman living in the New York Tri-State area. Heavily involved in theater at her college, she fulfills her passion for writing in poetry and short form story-writing. Currently, she is pursuing her BA in Chinese and AS in Business. Her goal is to develop a business network/production company that can help qtpoc artists pursue their art freely, while also using its funds to provide financial backing to twoc in financial crises.

About the Authors

Lulu Trujillo is a Latina Trans Woman from New Jersey, who is currently teaching English in Japan. She is currently trying to decide where in life to go, but for the mean time has decided to put all their energy into writing stories that can hopefully entertain people and teach them something new about the world. This is her first work published in an anthology and she is super excited to share more stories with readers in the future. Follow Lulu on tumblr and twitter for more writings and thoughts. Follow at lulus-library.tumblr.com and @Kokonoesensei

Saki is a stargazer and theorist. Find her on twitter @sayaendopeace.

Made in the USA
Columbia, SC
05 October 2018